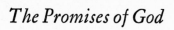

The Promises of God

The Promises of God

An Exercise in Biblical Thinking

by

CARROLL E. SIMCOX, Ph.D.

Assistant at Saint Thomas Church
New York City

242
SIM

MOREHOUSE-GORHAM CO.

NEW YORK

1958

PRINTED IN THE UNITED STATES OF AMERICA
BY THE HADDON CRAFTSMEN, INC., SCRANTON, PA.

To my friend
ROBERT BOLBACH
whose religion has the tang
of biblical salt

Preface

ANATOLE FRANCE sketches for us in *Penguin Island* a strange scene in heaven, in which St. Augustine takes God to task for an apparent change in God's mind and policy toward sinful men. God has grown more gentle and lenient, and the Saint views with alarm this sentimentality. God confesses apologetically: "Although my essence is immutable, the longer I live the more I incline to mildness. This change of character is evident to anyone who reads my two Testaments." This is M. France's characteristic whimsy which endears him to all freethinkers who have read a book or two but not the Bible itself. None the less, it reflects the view of many serious minds as to the two Testaments. Ages ago, the heretic Marcion roundly declared that the God of the Old Testament is the Devil of the New, and he proceeded to expurgate the Bible accordingly. By the time he had finished deleting those Scriptures which, in his mind, confused the diabolical with the divine, there wasn't much Bible left. Marcion's heresy has become the "orthodoxy" of many a modern Christian. The Old Testament is piously shunned and its God is ostracized—without a hearing—as no gentleman.

Marcion, France, and their fastidious partisans are wrong in their basic assumption about the Bible. Their mistake consists of taking each part of the Bible by itself, making it stand on its own feet, and requiring it to speak all by itself. Does the Book of Esther fail to mention the Name of God? Then it is a godless book; away with it. Does Ecclesiastes express a philosophy as nihilistic as modern French existentialism? Then it is no book for a God-fearing Christian and it must be kept out of the hands of our children. Does the bloodthirsty Jehovah of *I Samuel 15* behave as if He had not been required to memorize *I Corinthians 13* in Sunday School? Then take the latter and leave the former; clearly God has reformed Himself.

To read the Bible thus is to misread it utterly. The Church in drawing up the canon—selecting the contents—of the Bible never intended that it should be read piecemeal, but as a whole. And the organizing principle of the Bible as a whole (for Christians) is its witness to Christ in every one of its parts. Every Scripture either proclaims Christ or points to Him. Such a scandalous Scripture as Ecclesiastes points to Christ by pointing up the deadly emptiness and void in human life which Christ comes to fill. When Thackeray was writing *Vanity Fair* he told a friend that he was writing a book about people "without God in the world." He succeeded wonderfully well. The author of *Ecclesiastes* succeeds better, and his book belongs in the Bible as a truly inspired testimony to the nature of life *B.C.*—before Christ redeems it.

This is only one example. We could cite hundreds of others, and in this book we shall consider quite a number of them.

The Old Testament is pre-eminently the Book of man *B.C.,* before Christ comes into man's life. This is what gives Christian meaning and value, and above all truth, to everything in the Old Testament which scandalizes our ideas of divine goodness and human decency. If God is fierce against man in many Old Testament Scriptures it is because man unreconciled to God is sure to taste the fierceness of God. If we will not receive God's love through Christ we shall receive God's wrath. This, too, is revelation; this, too, is truth.

"Whatsoever things were written aforetime were written for our learning," says St. Paul, "that we through patience and comfort of the scriptures might have hope" (*Romans 15:4*). We cannot have hope in God until we have been brought to despair in man, or, to make it as personal as it ought to be, to despair in ourselves.

The Old Testament shows us man trying to find his way back to the Father and the home he has deserted. The New Testament shows us God coming all the way down into man's wilderness to find and to reclaim him. But before this can happen somebody must change his mind. Anatole France thought it was God. He would say—as so many have said—that the angry deity had to be reconciled to man. The precise opposite is true. Christ comes to change man's mind toward God. That is what needs changing.

God does not do this all at once. The Old Testament witnesses throughout to God's preparation of the world for the coming of Christ. This is what St. Augustine means by saying that the New Testament lies concealed in the Old and the Old Testament lies revealed in the New. It is a mystery but not a mystification. Christ is at work, in a hidden way, in the Old Testament. In the New Testament He casts aside His incognito and appears in the flesh.

Why not, then, read the New Testament only and leave the Old Testament to those who like to rummage around among those "old, far-off, unhappy things and battles long ago"? This seems a most reasonable question, but it oversimplifies everything. The truth is that *B.C.* does not stand for an ancient period of time now happily ended. We are still *B.C.* in our ordinary human works and ways—even we Christians. The Old Testament is the Book of man before he has been completely made over in the image of Christ—which makes it the Book of you and me. Adam in his self-assertion against God is you and I. Cain in his repudiation of responsibility for his brother is you and I. David in his lusting is you and I. Saul in his jealousy, Job in his complaining, Jacob in his scheming, Jonah in his self-righteousness, Rahab in her religion without morality, Ruth in her morality without religion—but why go on? Here we are on these ancient pages.

We see ourselves in the Old Testament, and we see God leading us on toward our end in Christ. We see Christ in the New Testament coming and taking hold of us and beginning His new creation in us. The New Testament takes us into the era of *A.D.* and it emphasizes that this era is only beginning in the days of the Apostles. It is still only beginning. As we have learned to put it today, we are still early Christians. "With God be the rest."

How to Use this Book

A word now about how to use this book. It is an exercise in what I consider a fruitful kind of biblical meditation. Here are eighty short chapters, short enough so that you can read two each day over a period of forty days: Lent, or any other season. They should be read in pairs. The first of each pair is based on some Old Testament passage, and is meant to show us ourselves in that aspect of our being which is *B.C.* Then, perhaps in the evening, you read the second chapter of the pair. This is based on a New Testament passage which points us toward our end in Christ and gives us some basis for judging how far into the era of *A.D.* we have moved.

These chapters are meant to stimulate your own meditation and discovery, not to "give the answers" in any final form. It is for God to give you "the answers" as fast as you show yourself ready to receive them.

C.E.S.

Contents

Contents 13

The Promises of God

1

In the Beginning God

In the beginning God created the heaven and the earth. And the earth was without form, and void; and darkness was upon the face of the deep. And the Spirit of God moved upon the face of the waters.
—*Genesis 1:1-2*

WHAT is the picture here, precisely? At first glance, one might answer: "Well, it is the picture of just nothing at all, except God; and of God saying 'Let there be'—and then there was something. This original something was shapeless and meaningless, but the organizing Spirit of God was brooding over all and beginning to bring order into chaos."

This is not wrong, but it is not enough. Most of us, when we think about the original creation, fix our imaginations upon the world in its beginning. But the proper object of attention is God, not the world. It is He who is in the beginning— in every beginning. The fundamental question about creation is not "What is the world like?" but "What is God like?" Is He good, bad, or indifferent? We have no basis for a judgment upon our world and our life in it until we have made up our minds about the character of God and His purposes for the world and for us.

You can put up with cancer, poverty, failure, injustice, death, and all the ills that flesh is heir to, if you can be sure that the Power and Mind and Purpose behind it all is good; that It means well, does well, and will make all things work together for good. The only ultimate question about anything is the question about God.

Genesis doesn't settle it all for us. It leaves us saying, with A. E. Housman, "How the world is managed, and why it was created, I cannot tell; but it is no feather-bed for the repose of sluggards." If this is all we know about it, it isn't very much.

In the beginning there is chaos. But we should note this well: even the chaos belongs to God. This is something to know. The chaos is not doomed to remain chaos forever, for there is One greater than the chaos in control of it and with plans of His own. Knowing this much, we come back to the question, Who is this mighty One behind the chaos? What is He like? What has He in mind for His world and for all that is in it, our own little creature selves included?

Genesis proclaims the existence, the reality, the controlling power of the mighty One behind it all. It leads us up to our next question: Who is He? What is His name, His character? What must we fear, what may we hope, from Him?

2

In the Beginning—the Word

In the beginning was the Word . . . And the Word was made flesh, and dwelt among us, and we beheld his glory.

—St. John 1:1, 14

GENESIS leaves us with the great question: What is God like? He creates the world, He orders and rules it. But to what end? The question is intimately personal as well as vastly cosmic; it is about us. Whatever God has in mind in creating the world He has in mind in creating me. His purpose for His creation is His purpose for me. If His purpose is cruel, or indifferent to the individual creature, so much the worse for me.

So I must know what God is like.

I find the answer I seek in Jesus Christ, the Word, the Self-expression of God to men.

St. John opens his version of the Gospel with a creation story obviously modeled upon the Genesis creation story. But it has one enormous difference: Christ. He is the answer to the question about God which Genesis leaves with us.

Christ is God's Self-disclosure. He is God showing Himself to us in such a way that He leaves no room for doubt or error in our minds as to what God is like. This is why we call Christ the Word of God. A word is a true word only as it reveals him who speaks it. In Christ, we do not see all that there is of

God; but all that we see in Christ is God, and it is enough for our present need. If my life is in the hands of a God like Christ I can rest content, and I need lose no sleep over what the world can do to me. It may misuse me, it may kill me; but this God is mightier than death, and His name and nature is love.

A little girl was afraid to go to sleep in the dark. Her fearfulness was a real agony. Her mother tried to reason her out of it one night by saying, "You know that you are not really alone in this dark bedroom. God is with you, and He is your protector." To this the child replied, with quivering lip, "I know that, but I want a protector with skin on!"

In her plea she was voicing the hope and fear of all humanity. We may believe that the great God who creates the world is our protector; but we want our protector "with skin on." Why? Primarily, so that we can see Him and know that He is *here* as well as *there*. But also, so that we can be sure that our divine Protector knows what it is to be "with skin on" like ourselves: to be capable of being afraid of the dark, to be capable of being hurt.

The Word becomes flesh, and we behold His glory. We see what God is like. He sees what human life is like—from the inside of our skin. And we can relax in the arms of such a God. We have our Protector with skin on, and we know that He has us.

3

The First Eve

And when the woman saw that the tree was good for food, and that
it was pleasant to the eyes, and a tree to be desired to make one wise,
she took of the fruit thereof, and did eat, and gave also unto her husband
with her; and he did eat.

—*Genesis 3:6*

DARE we censure our first mother very harshly? There is
nothing vicious in her that we can see, nothing depraved,
nothing deliberately anti-God or anti-man; at least, not as we
usually think of viciousness, depravity, and godlessness.

To be sure, God had commanded that she should not eat
of the fruit. It was His only commandment to date, and it was
not burdensome. But was it just? Was it reasonable? Eve
looked at the tree and wondered. It was "good for food,"
"pleasant to the eyes," and "to be desired to make one wise."
Thus it met man's practical need, his esthetic need, his intellectual need. What more can man want than the tree
offered? Food for the body, food for the soul's hunger for
beauty, food for the mind: the good, the beautiful, the true.
God is good. He wants His children to have these good things.
Then why not eat? Doesn't it simply make sense?

We find ourselves easily and honestly sympathizing with
Eve in her temptation, and for the simple reason that our
minds are warped as hers was. What ails her ails us.

The essence of Eve's sin (and ours) lies in seeking these good things on our own terms rather than on God's terms.

The satanic suggestion is that God has no right to be "unreasonable" and "arbitrary"—to say nay to *our* judgment of the reasonable and the right. Eve thought God's prohibition unworthy of God. Or, if the modern mind was in her (as it may well have been, for it is not really modern) she may have judged that God and man had somehow got their wires crossed on the subject. Maybe we had misunderstood God. Maybe this was an interpolation by a later editor of the sacred text; or a monkish invention; or a survival from primitive religion. She was all for a religion of love, not of fear! Religion is here to serve man, not man to serve religion. God is our friend and colleague, not our Lord and Master. Let us all sing bravely, "Courage, God, we come!" One must be reasonable in religion, and consider as divine commandment only that which serves the best interests of man—man being the judge of the same.

Eve did the brave, sensible, liberal thing: she ate. And her children have been in dire trouble ever since: with God, with one another, and with their own selves. Strange. Can it be that this fine liberal spirit is not enough?

4

The Second Eve

And Mary said, Behold the handmaid of the Lord; be it unto me according to thy word.

—*St. Luke 1:38*

THE Blessed Virgin is known as the second Eve, since in her the human race makes a new beginning. One may want to object that it is in Christ, rather than in His mother, that our broken humanity is made whole again and given a new life. This is of course true. But we cannot separate Christ from His mother. As Chesterton put it, those two heads are so close together that their haloes intermingle.

It was when Mary said "Be it unto me" that Christ's Incarnation and our redemption became possible. Mary is the only human being who ever gave anything to God. She gave humanity to God, at His request.

The first Eve fell because she did not take God's command seriously enough to obey it. It struck her as unreasonable. Who was God to be telling her what to do with her life? Wasn't her soul her own?

The glory of Mary is precisely that she does *not* call her soul her own. "Be it unto me according to *thy* word"—not mine. She is asked to do something far more "unreasonable," far more demanding and painful, than to abstain from eating some fruit. She is asked to bear a child without a human father, and to do so not knowing what the end of this strange venture will be. That it involves risk, pain, ridicule, misunderstanding, and nasty calumny is clear enough. But nothing else is clear—except that God asks it of her.

"Be it unto me according to thy word." God's will is all that she needs to know. And with her act of simple, absolute obedience our new creation begins.

The redeemed life, the life in Christ, is distinguished from the unredeemed life in Adam by just this difference: the children of the first Eve please themselves first, hoping that God approves; the children of the second Eve please God first, knowing that in the pain and peril of His service is their only peace, their only safety.

Hail, Mary, the Lord is with thee; and because He is with thee we dare to trust that He is with us, if we be found in thy Son, the Beloved.

5

The Curse of Knowledge

And the Lord God said, Behold, the man is become as one of us, to know good and evil: and now, lest he put forth his hand, and take also of the tree of life, and live for ever: therefore the Lord God sent him forth from the garden of Eden, to till the ground from whence he was taken.

—*Genesis 3:22-23*

I T IS a hard thing that God does to man, depriving him of the chance "to know good and evil." Again we find ourselves asking if God's action is reasonable. Doesn't God want us to know anything? Does He want us to spend our poor, short days miserably grubbing our livelihood from the soil, with never an upward look, a gracious holiday, an ecstasy of high thought or noble emotion? Apparently He does, if Genesis is to be believed. Ours is a hard fate, and hard is the heart of Him who decrees it.

We think about it thus because our minds are warped. This is fallen thinking.

Were we in our right minds, we should see that we have put this necessity upon God. We have forced Him to deal with us as we are. We have made it His hard duty as our loving Father to deprive us of knowledge, esthetic joy, and leisure for the pure contemplation of truth *until we have learned obedience to Him*.

Man can do his thinking and knowing either with God or

against Him. Man can know (with a warped knowledge) his
world and himself either "on his own," with no sense of his
dependence on God, or he can approach truth as did the great
pioneer of physics, Johannes Kepler. After each of his dis-
coveries Kepler would cry, "O God, I think thy thoughts after
thee!" God considers knowledge as safe in the hands of such
a man; and in no other hands. If we have trouble seeing God's
point, we may ponder the present-day terror of the knowledge
of nuclear fission. This knowledge is safe only if possessed by
saints.

God mercifully makes us subject to ignorance, to life at hard
labor, and to death, until we are ready for something better.
Christ comes to make us ready for the better thing.

Genesis leaves us in our painful but necessary bondage. We
are born, live, and die in this bondage. We rebel against it
but we accept it because we must. Our redemption begins when
we see God's loving purpose and long-range plan in it. He
wants to prepare us for something better—if we will be prepared. We must see our ignorance, weakness, and slavery, in
our fallenness, as the best that God can give us now. Our lot
becomes bearable, even bright with hope, if we can rise to see
it as the preparation for the knowledge, power, and glorious lib-
erty which is offered to us through Jesus Christ, the Lord of
the New Life.

6

The Blessing of Knowledge

And this is life eternal, that they might know thee the only true God, and Jesus Christ, whom thou hast sent.

—*St. John 17:3*

QUARRY the granite rock with razors, or moor the vessel with a thread of silk; then may you hope with such keen and delicate instruments as human knowledge and human reason to contend against those giants, the passion and the pride of man."[1] So wrote Newman. His contention is valid. Our passion and our pride are such an impregnable barrier to true knowledge that our best brains splinter and break against it. Not until our passion (self-will) and our pride (self-love) are removed, by a power mightier than our own, can we approach truth as it really is.

Christ declares in our text that we know truth only by knowing Him. He declares further that this knowledge of truth in Him is more than intellectual enlightenment; it is Life Eternal.

To grasp this we must see the immense difference between *saving knowledge* and *awareness of facts*.

We have saving knowledge when we know God as He is; for then we know what to do with the facts of life as we learn them. Factual knowledge is good if we know what to do with

[1] *The Idea of a University.*

it, but only then. A man may know that the earth circles the sun, that Homer was probably a syndicate, that it pays to advertise, and many other things animal and vegetable and mineral. But such knowledge does him no good until he knows what the God of truth wants him to do with it. It can do him grave harm. The man with facts in his head is a menace to his world, his neighbor, and himself unless he is taught by God how to use them wisely and constructively.

To know God means infinitely more than to have a sound theological view of Him. Theology is not knowing God; it is knowing about God. The knowledge of God which is Life Eternal is a twofold thing: it is acceptance of the vision of God which Christ gives us, and it is the absolute commitment of our lives to Him. Literally, to know God is to love Him. This knowledge is the Life Eternal—life in the Eternal. We do not know what it is to live until we have received this knowledge and have entered into this life in which God's will, rather than our own, moves our every thought, word, and deed.

A person who has this saving knowledge can be trusted with the awareness of facts; and God no longer withholds from him that knowledge of good and evil which is denied to all who are still in Adam—who live for themselves rather than for God.

7

Every Man for Himself

And the Lord said unto Cain, Where is Abel thy brother? And he said, I know not: Am I my brother's keeper?

—*Genesis 4:9*

THE modern Greek poet, Demetrios Capetanakis, represents Abel as speaking thus:

My brother Cain, the wounded, liked to sit
Brushing my shoulder, by the staring water
Of life, or death, in cinemas half-lit
By scenes of peace that always turned to slaughter.

He liked to talk to me. His eager voice
Whispered the puzzle of his bleeding thirst,
Or prayed me not to make my final choice,
Unless we had a chat about it first.

And then he chose the final pain for me.
I do not blame his nature: he's my brother;
Nor what you call the times: our love was free,
Would be the same at any time; but rather

The ageless ambiguity of things
Which makes our life mean death, our love be hate.
My blood that streams across the bedroom sings:
"I am my brother opening the gate!"[1]

[1] *Abel,* by Demetrios Capetanakis. From *The Shores of Darkness.* The Devin-Adair Company, New York, 1949. Used by permission.

It is a lovely vision of a Christ-like Abel redeeming his murdering brother by his own blood and his own forgiveness. But the Christian reader must not be deceived. We can forgive our wrongdoers, but we cannot redeem them. We can be forgiven by our brother; we cannot be redeemed by him.

Cain needs to be not only forgiven but cured. And the cure can be wrought only by God. Cain's sickness is everyman's sickness, and the cure he needs everyman needs. His trouble is his total individualism, his working principle that in this world it is every man for himself. This is commonly accepted as the natural philosophy for the natural man. Doesn't Nature write this law large and plain across our landscape? Isn't this the very condition of existence? If you don't look out for yourself, who will? Surely, it is putting it pretty stiffly to say that a man who lives by this necessary rule is a murderer at heart. Cain must have something worse wrong with him than this.

Such we call our natural reasoning. Our constant appeal to Nature, rather than to God, as our moral teacher, betrays our fallenness. Nature, as we see it, justifies our doing whatever we want with our brother to our own advantage. The tiger lives, the lamb dies so that the tiger may live; it is entirely natural—*dulce et decorum*—to want to live; *ergo*. . . .

But God created man in His own image, that is, as a being who lives above Nature when he is true to his true self. The law of the jungle is not the law of man—when man is right. Man has a God-given nature, indeed; it is higher than Nature.

Cain is man gone wrong at the root of his being. No wonder he murders.

Every man for himself. This is the recognized law for men, for corporations, for nations, in the world as we know it. But is this life or death?

8

Members One of Another

For by one Spirit are we all baptized into one body, whether we be
Jews or Gentiles, whether we be bond or free; and have been all made
to drink into one Spirit. For the body is not one member, but many.
. . . And whether one member suffer, all the members suffer with it; or
one member be honoured, all the members rejoice with it. Now ye are
the body of Christ, and members in particular.

—I Corinthians 12:13-14, 26-27

YOU don't keep out of trouble by becoming a Christian;
you get into it: and not only your own troubles, but those
of all the other members of Christ. Their troubles and their
triumphs become yours. In the Body of Christ, Cain's question
is answered with an emphatic affirmative: I am my brother's
keeper, and he is mine.

The vivid awareness of being a living member of Christ
creates a sense of the connaturality of all human life. What this
means was expressed by the words, and still more by the works,
of John Woolman, the American Quaker saint of the eight-
eenth century, a pioneer of the movement to free the slaves.
He looked upon his world and he testified:

I saw a mass of matter of a dull gloomy color between the North
and the East, and was informed that this mass was human beings,
in as great misery as they could be, and live; and that I was mixed
up with them and henceforth I must not consider myself as a dis-
tinct or separate being.

A far cry, this, from Cain! And a long distance.

This is the new life in Christ. This is man coming into his own again.

Professor Arnold Toynbee sees writ large one essential truth of the Gospel in all human history, and he declares that "the only society in which there can be a harmony of wills is one in which two or three—or two or three thousand million—are gathered together in God's name with God Himself in the midst of them. In a society including the One True God as well as His human creatures, God plays a unique part. He is a party to the relation between each human member and Himself; but in virtue of this He is also a party to the relations between each human member, and through this participation of God, breathing His own divine love into human souls, human wills can be reconciled."[1]

Toynbee makes it a triangular relationship: God at the apex and you and your neighbor at the ends of the base. St. Paul's metaphor of the body makes it much closer than that. If we are in Christ we are in one another. So much so that if my neighbor suffers, Christ suffers in him and I suffer in Christ, because we three are *one life*—drinking of one Spirit. In Christ I am more than my brother's keeper. I am he; he is I; and we are Christ.

[1] From *A Study of History* (vol. VII, p. 510) by Arnold J. Toynbee, published by Oxford University Press under the auspices of the Royal Institute of International Affairs.

9

The Man Who Walked with God

And Enoch walked with God: and he was not; for God took him.
—*Genesis 5:24*

THE awareness of personal immortality is not a dominant note in the Old Testament, but to say that it is not there is to say far too much. Here is this lovely tribute to Enoch as evidence. It does not suggest that God annihilated him, or let him languish miserably in some gloomy land of shades. God *took* him. Enoch went to be with God.

To be sure, it is said that Enoch "was not." In the eyes of men he had ceased to be. But there is clear recognition here that our being, our existence, stands not in man's observation but in God's observation. We live so long as God sees us.

The text declares that Enoch's loving companionship with God was not destroyed, but deepened, at his death. A little girl in Sunday School once told the story in these words: "Enoch and God used to take long walks together. And one day they walked further than usual; and God said, 'Enoch, you must be tired; come into My house and rest!'" She had apprehended the spirit and the sense of the text.

Enoch begins his immortal life with God by walking with God in his mortal life. In this way he learns his own immortality. He comes to know God by loving Him, obeying Him, communing with Him, seeking His will to do it. It may be that in his sceptical youth he thinks of God and immortality only as the "Grand Perhaps"; but, like young Donald Hankey many ages later, he is willing to bet his life on God. So he puts his hand out into the infinite space and the eternal silence; and the Hand of Another takes it.

It is only through such loving knowledge of God, begun in intimate companionship born of faith and trust, that any person comes to know his own immortality. Whether we live forever or die forever cannot be settled by our science or philosophy. But if we know God as Enoch knows Him we are given the invincible assurance that He will not leave us in the dust.

When the little girl imagined God as saying to Enoch, "Come into My house and rest!" she was drawing upon a knowledge which had not been given to men in Enoch's day. She was a Christian; and in this matter the simplest Christian has been shown more, hence knows more, than the wisest pre-Christian saint could ever know. Genesis has nothing to say of the Father's House of Many Mansions. But it has something to say about God: that He is our Father. To know this, to the full, is to know our immortality.

10

The God Who Walked with Man

In my Father's house are many mansions: if it were not so, I would
have told you. I go to prepare a place for you.
—*St. John 14:2*

ENOCH was the man who walked with God. In the course
of his walking with God, in faith and love, he was given
to know that God loved him too much to let him cease to be.
Jesus is the God who walked with man. We all cherish His
words about the Father's House of Many Mansions; but these
words can bring no assurance to us except as we realize that
He knows what He is talking about. If this is only another
man's beautiful guess about the hereafter, that is all it is—another guess. Jesus claims to speak as one who knows. "If it
were not so, *I* would have told you. *I* go to prepare a place for
you."

Among Christ's sayings this is not only one of the loveliest,
it is one of the most easily misunderstood. One of Galsworthy's
characters, Aunt Juley Forsyte, loved this text. "It always com-
forted her with its suggestion of house property, which had
made the fortune of dear Roger. The Bible was a great re-
source, and then on very fine Sundays, there might be church,
if there were nothing else to do."[1]

Aunt Juley had not bothered to ascertain what the text

[1] John Galsworthy, *The Man of Property.* Charles Scribner's Sons, New York, 1906.
Used by permission.

means. Had she done so, she would have found it less comforting. She might have noted that the Father's House is the *Father's* House, not another handsome piece of Forsyte property. If we get to heaven we are not going to own it. We shall be God's guests, entirely dependent upon His hospitality. We shall possess nothing in heaven; we shall be possessed.

In fact, the whole world, temporal and eternal, is the Father's House. We are in it now; and as His guests. The Many Mansions of which Jesus speaks are not palatial houses, as our modern use of the word "mansions" suggests. They are best thought of as resting-places along our way. We are on a journey, and our final goal is a perfect at-home-ness with God. As Jesus gives His beloved promise He is saying that He goes on ahead of us to prepare a place for us at the end of each day's journey. He knows the way perfectly. He knows what we shall need along the way, and He will provide for each need as it arises. Hence if we simply follow Him we cannot go wrong. And when we come to die, we shall find that He has provided for this too: He has passed this way before us: and He beckons us to walk into the forbidding stream as He calls from the other side: "Don't be afraid. I have already crossed it. I am over here waiting for you."

11

Giants in the Earth

There were giants in the earth in those days.

—Genesis 6:4

THE opening of the sixth chapter of Genesis is a strange story about the Nephilim, a race of demi-gods born of union between the "sons of God" and the "daughters of men." This remnant of a prehistoric Semitic myth is an incongruity in the Bible, contradicting the basic biblical tenet of the absolute gulf between God and man. These "giants in the earth" are half-divine, half-human, and why they were not edited out by scribes of a later age is a mystery. But the phrase "giants in the earth" has been lifted out of its original context and made a proverb. When we want to talk about the good old days, when men were men, we exclaim, "There were giants in the earth in those days!" We mean that the best men are pigmies now.

We have always done this. We have always looked back wistfully to the brave days of old with their peerless men and their pure women. There is a reasonable and right way of doing this which is wholesome. The remembrance of the great souls of times past is one of the vital tonics by which our souls are stimulated toward greatness. But this complaint that the men of old were giants while we are pigmies both paralyzes our growth and reproaches our Maker. If God sets before us gi-

gantic tasks but gives us only pigmy strength with which to
do them, He is guilty of injustice and folly.

What is most noteworthy, however, in this glorification of
the superman of old is its normal disregard for moral character and spiritual maturity. Those old-time giants of our ad-
miring fancy are men who, we say, could stand on their own
feet—could take it—could carve their own destinies. They were
leonine. They were beyond and above the Sunday School morality of pale young curates and feeble old ladies. Supermen,
not milksops! Brave, bold, creative, and free, not timid slaves
of conscience and convention.

What we glorify in them is not their goodness but their brute
strength. (I am speaking of course of the usual form this fan-
tasy takes.) The giants of our sentimental journey back into
history appear gigantic to us because they were so successfully
self-assertive, greedy, and cruel. Had we been their contemporaries we should have dreaded and loathed them. Across the
haze of years they appear romantically stark, strong, and
wholly enviable.

The question we should ask and settle in our minds about
any giant of the past is: What makes a giant in our eyes? Who
qualifies: Herod or Simeon? Paul or Nero? Ghenghis Kahn
or Francis?

There were giants in the earth in those days, armed with
only the sword of the Spirit; and there were pigmies in the
earth in those days, armed with iron chariots and big sticks.
We must make up our minds first, and rightly, as to who were
the giants.

12

The New Kind of Giant

If any man be in Christ, he is a new creature.

—*II Corinthians 5:17*

ALEXANDER THE GREAT and Paul the Apostle are both world conquerors. Both are bold, venturesome, imaginative geniuses. The distinction between them cannot be stated by saying simply that one genius was bad and the other good. Alexander was not an eminently bad man, as bad men come. Paul was a woefully defective saint, as well he knew. We see here two different kinds of giants, who are incommensurable because they are spiritually of different species.

Canon B. H. Streeter remarked that the coming of Christ wrought a mighty revolution in man's thinking about God: slowly through the ages, but inevitably, men think of God less and less in terms of Caesar and more and more in terms of Christ. This is true, and it profoundly affects man's thinking about man as well.

Our Christian view is that the giant is the Christ-like man. The giant is strong as he is like Christ, weak as he is unlike Christ.

The literary ex-communist, Arthur Koestler, looking at the menace confronting the world today, declares that "neither the saint nor the revolutionary can save us; only the synthesis of

the two."[1] We know what he means, and we agree. But there
lurks in this definition the old fear that the saint is incompe-
tent for revolutionary work because he is a saint. Another
literary man, Clifton Fadiman, betrays the same misunderstanding in his remarks that "no saint has ever been a good
literary critic."[2] He should read Augustine, Clement of Alex-
andria, Jerome, and many of the uncanonized "saints," ancient and modern, to see what sanctification does to sharpen
the critical faculty. Mr. Fadiman assumes that the saint cannot
think critically, with intelligent discrimination, without ceas-
ing to think spiritually.

The truth is that most of us need thorough re-education on
this point. The new man in Christ is enabled to work with his
head and his hands as he never could otherwise. Soft-hearted-
ness and soft-headedness are not synonyms. The new man in
Christ thinks to the glory of God, and therefore he thinks.
And in action against evil he is a tough and resourceful fighter
because he is convinced that God and he are always a majority.
With this faith he is the only giant in the earth.

[1] Arthur Koestler, *The Yogi and the Commissar*. The Macmillan Company, New
York, 1945. Used by permission of the publisher.

[2] Clifton Fadiman, *Party of One*. Used by permission of World Publishing Company,
Cleveland.

13

Is God a Fumbler?

And God saw that the wickedness of man was great in the earth, and that every imagination of the thoughts of his heart was only evil continually. And it repented the Lord that he had made man on the earth, and it grieved him at his heart.

—Genesis 6:5-6

A S WE read through the early chapters of Genesis and we come to this preface to the story of Noah we are sure to be a bit startled. Here is God making a whole elaborate world for man to live in, making man to be the major-domo of it all, then deciding that He has made a stupid mistake. One thinks of a painter working for months on a canvas, then looking at his finished work and in a fury of disappointment taking a knife and ripping it all to tatters, cursing himself as a bungling fool. Can it be that God once felt this way about His creature man, for whom He had such high hopes in the beginning?

It is disturbing enough to have it suggested that God changes His mind in this petulant way when He sees that man is a mess. It is even more disturbing to be told that God cannot control His own experiment. He creates man, hoping that man will choose to be good, but giving man the power to choose evil; and man chooses to be bad; and God is helpless in face of this disappointing development. His experiment with man has apparently got out of control. God can do nothing except call the whole thing off, to destroy His mistake by destroying man.

This seems to be the word of Genesis, and we hate to think that it is the last word on the subject. In justice to Genesis we should remember what follows. God does not destroy the whole human race. He finds one good man, Noah, in the whole sorry lot, and He keeps humanity going through Noah and his progeny. But Noah's progeny fall into the same old evil ways. If God's idea is to correct His experiment in this way He fails here too, and thus God's incompetence continues from generation to generation.

Is it really true that God is powerless to deal with human iniquity and to correct His work? If all that we have as evidence is Genesis, this must be our conclusion. But we have something else to ponder: the great intervention of God in Christ. There *is* something else God can do, in His dilemma, and in Jesus Christ He does it. He does not need to correct His "mistake" by burying it. He has an alternative: He can actually become His own "mistake," man. And in so doing He can convert His "mistake" into His most glorious achievement.

14

The Perfect Correction

God was in Christ, reconciling the world unto himself, not imputing their trespasses unto them. . . . For he hath made him to be sin for us, who knew no sin; that we might be made the righteousness of God in him.

—II Corinthians 5:19, 21

A MAN is never a bungler at his job if he can correct his own mistakes. But then no man can make perfect correction of his mistakes. This is beyond man's power. The nearest approach to such perfect correction that I know of is commonly done by Persian rug-makers. The rug-maker stands in front of a perpendicular frame, pushing the heavy thread through with a needle as he tries to work his pattern into the fabric. Once the needle goes through at any point, it cannot be pulled back. The mistake is woven permanently into the rug. But if the rug-maker is a first-class artist, he knows what to do next: he alters his original design to include the mistake, and the result may well be a more beautiful rug than was originally projected.

This is a parable, of a sort, of God's creative dealing with His "mistake"—man. Once man has sinned, the mistake is somehow permanent. Not even God can "make as if" it had not happened. The world cannot be the same as it was before the sin. But God can work the sin into the altered thing in

43

such a way that the whole is not ruined. God is more than competent to turn man's sin into divine success.

Of course, our parable ceases to be a true parable—that is, likeness—at the most crucial point. The rug-maker is dealing with his own mistake. He makes the mistake himself, and whatever he does with it the mistake is his own. In the case of man's sinning, the "mistake"—a ludicrously mild word for it—is not God's, but man's.

Even so, only God can cope with it. And He does this in the way described by St. Paul in very stark and startling language. Christ *becomes* sin for us—He who knows no sin of his own—so that we might be made the righteousness of God in Him. God becomes His own "mistake"! Man did it, but God in Christ takes upon Himself the responsibility, the guilt, and the punishment. Some people call the whole idea of the crucifixion of the innocent Christ for us—in our place—something immoral and unjust. Let us understand that so long as we think of this divine Thing in terms of "justice" and "fair play" we cannot hope to comprehend it or to make sense of it. We must approach it considering only God's love and God's hopes and plans for His children. We have gone wrong. He wants to put us right. We cannot put ourselves right. The real work of correction can be done only by God. So Christ comes down, takes upon Himself our death, and gives us His life. Thus the perfect correction is made.

15

Babel

And the whole earth was of one language, and of one speech. . . .
And the Lord said, Behold, the people is one, and they have all one
language. . . . Go to, let us go down, and there confound their language,
that they may not understand one another's speech.

—*Genesis 11:1, 6-7*

WHAT God does at Babel seems another of those hard
things He does to His children. There we were: all one
people, of one language; one big family, if not a happy one.
And God says, Enough of this. He confounds our language and
splits us into ten thousand tribes and tongues, cultures and
kindreds.

This ancient tale describes our real human situation. There
is more than one iron curtain; there are thousands. The American businessman, the Russian commissar, the Chinese coolie,
the South African housewife, all live on the same small planet,
but a hundred big barriers separate them. We bewail this
bitterly. Alas, if only we could get together! If only we spoke
one language of mind and heart and lips and life! So we look
wistfully to the UN and the UNESCO and all such efforts to
pull together our shattered race, hoping and praying that they
might succeed.

It is right that we should. Yet it is God who visits upon us
this terrible disunity, *in His love:* to prevent us from doing
worse things with our powers than we can now do.

When my brother and I were small boys we were as brotherly at times as Kilkenny cats, and when our parents could not stand the strife of tongues any longer they took remedial action. One of us was sent to the attic and the other to the basement. With intercommunication between us no longer possible, peace for everybody else was possible.

The great world of grown-up people is not as grown-up as it thinks. Men and nations are not to be trusted with a closer community than they have. We force God to take His separating action, which He does by confounding our language and by otherwise separating us from each other so that we cannot disturb the peace of His world to an intolerable degree. In this state of dividedness we must remain until we are ready to behave as mature, law-abiding children of God.

God turned Babel into babble very early in our history, and He has allowed us to suffer long in our world of confusion. But He has opened to us a road to unity and community, through Jesus Christ our Lord. This we shall consider in our next meditation.

16

Babel Undone

And they were all filled with the Holy Ghost, and began to speak
with other tongues, as the Spirit gave them utterance. And there were
dwelling at Jerusalem Jews, devout men, out of every nation under
heaven. Now when this was noised abroad, the multitude came together,
and were confounded, because that every man heard them speak in his
own language.

—Acts 2:4-6

A T BABEL, God acts to divide men. At Pentecost, He acts
to unite men. Devout men "out of every nation under
heaven" could understand these simple Galilean Christians
as they proclaimed the wonderful works of God in Christ. In
receiving the Spirit of God they received this astounding power
to be understood by everybody. Pentecost is the undoing of
Babel. The Pentecost story shows us what happens when men
receive the Spirit of Christ: out of many they are made one.
The barriers fall, the walls collapse, and heart speaks to heart
in the very language of heaven.

Pentecost is not an ancient isolated event. It is what happens
in us when we are born again and receive the Spirit. We become the kind of people whom God can trust and use. No
longer need we be scattered for the peace and safety of the
world. God dares to let us unite, and He unites us. We begin to
speak that new language, the language which every human
heart instantly understands and receives with joy: the language
of love.

For the Holy Spirit is the love of God poured into our hearts. And it is only by the Spirit's working, by the love of God in us, that the barriers between man and man can be broken down. Love is the language that everybody understands, the force that breaks down all barriers, the unifying agent which makes all men one in Christ.

Dr. Schweitzer tells how it is when some African native is brought to him suffering from one of those frightful jungle diseases. After the doctor has alleviated the poor fellow's pain, the man reaches for his hand and will not let it go. The doctor then tells him how the Lord Jesus has told the doctor and his wife to come down there to heal sick Africans. He writes: "The African sun is shining through the coffee bushes into the dark shed, but we black and white sit side by side and feel that we know by experience the meaning of the words: 'And all ye are brethren.' "[1] Black African and white European then see "eye to eye" because they see heart to heart; and they see heart to heart because the Light of the Holy Spirit shines between them. Upon them the curse of Babel lies no more, and the blessing of Pentecost has come down as the rain of heaven upon the mown grass.

[1] Albert Schweitzer, *On the Edge of the Primeval Forest*. The Macmillan Company, New York, 1931. Used by permission of the publisher.

17

Ten Righteous Men

And Abraham drew near, and said, Wilt thou also destroy the righteous with the wicked? Peradventure there be fifty righteous within the city: wilt thou also destroy and not spare the place for the fifty righteous that are therein? That be far from thee to do after this manner, to slay the righteous with the wicked: and that the righteous should be as the wicked, that be far from thee: Shall not the Judge of all the earth do right?

—Genesis 18:23-25

GOD seems to find Abraham's passionate pleading for the wicked city of Sodom irresistible. Under Abraham's unrelenting examination, God finally concedes that the city should be spared if there be as many as ten righteous men in it. This would be "right," according to Abraham; and "shall not the Judge of all the earth do right?"

Several facts should be noted about this story. Sodom is not a city of Israel, yet Israel's God is seen as the God of Sodom with power over it to spare or to destroy. Jehovah is coming into His own as God of all the earth.

Then there is manifest in the story a realization of the value and saving power of the lone righteous individual in an unrighteous society. If there are no more than ten righteous men in Sodom, few though they be they still hold the reins of real power. Their goodness may save the city from its doom. Never underestimate the preserving and leavening power of plain goodness in a world both very big and very bad.

And the picture of Abraham the pleader and intercessor for sinners is noble and exalting, a true type of that glory which shall be revealed ages later in Him who, by His intercession with the Father, taketh away the sin of the world.

But Sodom was destroyed, in the end; and we must believe that the Judge of all the earth did right. For there were not so many as ten righteous men in it, or even one. There never is a righteousness of men which can save, for there is no such righteousness which is pure enough. Abraham was trusting in the righteousness of the few relatively good men in Sodom, rather than in that righteousness of God which is His love. There are always some relatively good men—men less bad than others. But this is the most that can be said for the best of men. Such goodness as they have is very precious and very powerful; but if a city or society or world is to be saved, it must be by a righteousness which is not in men but only in God.

Ten righteous men are not enough, nor are ten million. Our only hope is in the one righteous God.

18

No Righteous Men

For when we were yet without strength, in due time Christ died for the ungodly. For scarcely for a righteous man will one die: yet peradventure for a good man some would even dare to die. But God commendeth his love toward us, in that, while we were yet sinners, Christ died for us. Much more then, being now justified by his blood, we shall be saved from wrath through him. For if, when we were enemies, we were reconciled to God by the death of his Son, much more, being reconciled, we shall be saved by his life.

—Romans 5:6-10

ST. PAUL is not easy reading, and his Epistle to the Romans is his most difficult writing—and his greatest. In it he works out his doctrine of *justification by faith*. This is not Paul's doctrine in the sense of his invention; it is the Gospel, expressed in Paul's life and language.

In the passage now before us he gives us a fairly simple statement of the doctrine. Christ died for us at a time when we had no real righteousness in us at all, when we were "yet without strength." There was not a single righteous man upon the earth. Had some of us been reasonably good, by Christ's standard, His dying for us would then be understandable as the sacrifice He was willing to make for deserving friends. But God's love for us, which acts through Christ, does not wait until we are worthy of it.

We are justified—accepted by God—not by our worth to Him but by His love for us. Our Chinese contemporary, Dr.

Lin Yutang, scoffs at the idea of hell by saying that we are literally "not worth a damn" to God. He can make a good case for that, if all that we are looking at is our own cosmic importance and moral worth. But the Christian has something else to take into account. He sees in Christ the disclosure of a divine love for us which is beyond all understanding. We are "worth a damn" to God—even worth His dying for us, for reasons known only to Himself. His love for us, rather than our merits, gives us our confidence that we are accepted by Him. This is justification by faith, and it would be more accurately described as justification by God's love for us.

When we see God's love in action for us on Calvary we who "were enemies" are "reconciled" to Him as His penitent and adoring children. We begin to be "saved" when we begin to live and act in the spirit of Isaac Watts' lines:

> Were the whole realm of nature mine,
> That were a present far too small;
> Love so amazing, so divine,
> Demands my soul, my life, my all.[1]

We must first be reconciled to God. Our acceptance of Christ's death as the revelation of God's love does this for us. Then we live out our gratitude and our answering love, and we are "saved by his life" if we persevere to the end.

[1] No. 337, *The Hymnal 1940.*

19

God Will Provide a Lamb. I.

And Abraham said, My son, God will provide himself a lamb for a
burnt offering. . . .

—Genesis 22:8

ONE should read the whole of Genesis 22 for an understanding of this text. It seems to us a grim story, hardly
creditable to either God or Abraham. What kind of God is He
who makes such cruel trial of His faithful servent? And what
kind of man is he who will offer his own child to God? What
kind of murderous fanaticism is this, calling itself "faith" and
"true religion"? Such questions the modern mind is bound to
ask, even if it has in it some biblical religion. It is repelled
rather than attracted by what it sees of both God and Abraham
in the Genesis story.

For Christians, the rest of the story is to be found in the
Gospel. Before coming to that, however, we should sit down
with the Genesis story and calmly try to understand it as it
stands. It is the testing of Abraham by the severest test that can
be applied to a man. He is asked to give his dearest possession,
his beloved child, to God. He takes the boy up into a mountain
and prepares the altar. As Isaac sees the fire and the knife he
knows that a sacrifice is in the offing, but he does not know
that he is the intended victim. He asks where is the animal to
be killed, and Abraham answers, "My son, God will provide
himself a lamb."

53

Is Abraham saying this to allay Isaac's fears, as a kindly deception, or does he believe it himself: that God will provide at the last minute a substitute for Isaac? We have no way of finding out. But he is sure that God will provide a suitable object for sacrifice. If it must be Isaac, so be it. In that case, Isaac will be the lamb which God provides.

Isaac is very dear to Abraham, but God is dearer. This is Abraham's love for God. If God requires the offering of Isaac, this will be the best thing possible. This is Abraham's faith in God. If we cannot comprehend such love and faith, if our religion is more "restrained" and "reasonable," so much the worse for us and for our religion.

"My son, God will provide himself a lamb." God does. So the story has a happy ending, though not an entirely conclusive one. What has been established by it is simply that God has a right to ask of us our dearest and best, and the test of our faith and love is whether we are willing to give it to Him.

One thing more, and this Abraham saw and we need to see: Isaac was not Abraham's, but God's. Nobody, nothing, is our own; everybody, everything, is His: even our children.

20

God Will Provide a Lamb. II.

The next day John seeth Jesus coming unto him, and saith, Behold the Lamb of God, which taketh away the sin of the world.
—*St. John 1:29*

THE lamb is a biblical symbol with diverse meanings, and we cannot consider them all. In our present text, two meanings in particular are uppermost: first, God provides the Lamb of God, Christ, as He provides the ram in place of Isaac in the case of Abraham's sacrifice; and, second, this Lamb whom God now provides in the person of Christ is able to take away the sin of the world.

We noted that Abraham had nothing strictly his own to offer to God, neither Isaac nor the beast. We have no Christ of our own to offer to God. The Father must provide His eternally beloved Son to be our saving Sacrifice, which is to say that we are dependent upon God for everything in our salvation. We cannot achieve our own reconciliation to God. We can only accept it, as wrought by Him.

By the time John came, it had become clear to the people of God that the blood of bulls and goats and sheep could not take away the sin of the world. It had been tried for ages, and the sin of the world remained.

So, in the fullness of time, God sends forth His Son who can indeed take away the sin of the world. This Lamb is none other than the eternal Son of God, of one substance with the Father. He takes all the sin of the world upon Himself and carries it to His death and to its death.

Yes, we say, this is the Christian story, and there never was a story like it. But has the sin of the world really been taken away? Does not Fra Lippo Lippi see things as they are only too well?

> First, every sort of monk, the black and white,
> I drew them, fat and lean: then, folk at church,
> From good old gossips waiting to confess
> Their cribs of barrel-droppings, candle-ends,—
> To the breathless fellow at the altar-foot,
> Fresh from his murder, safe and sitting there
> With the little children round him in a row
> Of admiration, half for his beard and half
> For that white anger of his victim's son
> Shaking a fist at him with one fierce arm,
> Signing himself with the other because of Christ
> (Whose sad face on the cross sees only this
> After the passion of a thousand years) . . .

Browning's cynical artist sees the Passion of Christ as powerless through a thousand years to cure people of their sinning, and so we all see it—until we see all the way into it. These sinning Christians in the church, whatever their formal beliefs about it, have not *accepted* Christ's redemption and been conformed to it. Christ has died for them, but He does not fully live in them. Where He rules, the power of sin is broken; and after the Passion of two thousand years this is still true.

21

Jacob's Ladder

And Jacob went out from Beersheba, and went toward Haran. And he lighted upon a certain place, and tarried there all night, because the sun was set; and he took of the stones of that place, and put them for his pillows, and lay down in that place to sleep. And he dreamed, and behold a ladder set up on the earth, and the top of it reached to heaven: and behold the angels of God ascending and descending on it.

—Genesis 28:10-12

JACOB had been a swindler and a sharp practitioner. Then he had become a wanderer: not necessarily because of his evil-doings, for better men than he can suffer exile and homelessness. But even if he does not see his fate in terms of punishment for his earlier misdeeds, his inner guilt and his outer adversity combine to trouble his sleep.

His dream is of a ladder stretched between earth and heaven, with angels ascending and descending upon it. Now, dreams are most mysterious things, unless we accept Freud's neat scheme of interpreting them which makes any dream as plain as mud. To most of us it seems much more rational to let the mystery remain mysterious.

Jacob's dream, however, explains itself. He sees a ladder between heaven and earth which means that God can come down to man and man can go up to God. The angels ascending carry man's prayers to God, the angels descending bring God's answers to man.

The dream is the decisive turning point in Jacob's life. Henceforth he is God's man. He has seen the God who hears and answers prayer, who builds the ladder between heaven and earth. His vision of God transforms him into God-likeness, as it always does and must. To see God is to be changed.

Jacob had learned from his own failure that he could not be a good man or even a decent man by his own moral effort. And he had cut himself off from God by his own most grievous fault. He could build no ladder of his own by which to climb back into his broken communion with God. Yet a ladder there must be, between God in heaven and this frail child of dust on earth. God builds the ladder. God makes it possible for us to come to Him and for Him to come to us.

The coming of Christ is many long ages in the future when Jacob has his dream; but in his ladder Christ is promised and prefigured. One day the dream will come true in the flesh. But no man can receive the gift of Christ until first he sees what Jacob sees: that the distance between God and man is very great; that there must be a ladder; and that only God can build it.

22

Jacob's Dream Come True

Verily, verily, I say unto you, Hereafter ye shall see heaven open,
and the angels of God ascending and descending upon the Son of man.
—*St. John 1:51*

IN THIS strange, literally fantastic, statement, Jesus recalls Jacob's dream of the ladder and tells His first fol-
lowers that they are going to see the ancient dream fullfilled
before their eyes—in the Son of man. Christ Himself is the
ladder. His friends are already astonished by the great things
they have seen in Him, but they have seen nothing yet.

He uses the term "Son of man" here rather than "Son of
God." This Son-of-man terminology is one of the puzzling
things in the Gospel, with varying shades of meaning which
are often hard for us to pin-point; but one of the more fixed
and constant meanings is that "Son of God" expresses Christ's
deity and "Son of man" His humanity. Both are necessary to
convey the whole truth about Him, that He is true God and
true man. "Son of man" is the right word in this case, because
it is in virtue of His humanity that Christ the divine "Ladder"
reaches all the way down from God to where we are, reaches
us on the very ground level of our life and being.

Chesterton described Christ's characteristic type of metaphor
as gigantesque. The one we have here is typically so: the God-
Man is a ladder, and angels ascend and descend upon His
human figure. A less extravagant figure of speech would not

tax the imagination so much, but neither would it convey so much of the glorious meaning and truth of God's gift of Christ to us.

As Jacob saw in his dream, so is it in the dream come true: God provides the ladder Himself. Man does nothing to create Christ or to merit Him. He is God's pure gift, and only so can man receive Him: without pride, without any sense that we have earned what He brings to us.

The angels of prayer and penitence and hope pass from us to God. The angels of mercy and forgiveness and love pass from God to us. Christ is indeed the ladder by which these ministering angels pass between heaven and earth. He is the living ladder—the Mediator.

No longer need we dream of a ladder between heaven and earth whereby God might come to us and we might climb to Him. We have Jacob's dream come true: Christ the Mediator, God's way to man and man's way to God. The great gulf is bridged.

23

Work Made Tolerable

And Jacob served seven years for Rachel; and they seemed unto him but a few days, for the love he had to her.

—*Genesis 29:20*

YOUNG Jacob did not enjoy working any more than do we, and before we go deeper into his case we should make an honest confession: When we say that we love our work, most of us are saying what we think we ought to feel rather than what we actually feel. Most work is not fun for most people. The Bible regards man's daily toil as a burden, and tells us that our work is hard and grievous to us because we are sinners and our toil is the punishment of our sin. An honest self-analysis will show the truth of this. What makes our work a burden grievous to be borne is our self-love, our self-concern, which is our sin. We say that when a person can "forget himself" in his work he will be happy, and we are right. But how hard it is to forget ourselves!

Insofar as we are normal human beings and not redeemed saints we hate to work; not because we are lazy but because we are self-concerned. Our work ceases to be a burden only when it becomes a cause; and a cause is by definition something in which we can find ourselves by losing ourselves—which is to say, in which we can rise above our sin.

Jacob wanted Rachel as his wife, and her father Laban would not let him have her for the asking. Jacob must work for seven hard, long years. But "they seemed unto him but a few days, for the love he had to her." It was his love for Rachel, not his love for God, which gave Jacob such a glorious lift and made the years race as he toiled. It did not make his work joyful, but it made it tolerable and much less burdensome than it would have been otherwise.

To love the person or thing for which one works in this way, be it one's lady or family or country or art or cause, is to be emancipated from drudgery. When love for another replaces love for self as our motivation, we enter into this freedom from drudgery.

How can we get this, if we do not have it? There is only one way: by finding somebody or something which we can love more dearly than we love ourselves, and working for that. It is the only cure for the misery and slavery of unredeemed work.

24

Work Made Joyful

For our light affliction, which is but for a moment, worketh for us a far more exceeding and eternal weight of glory; while we look not at the things which are seen, but at the things which are not seen: for the things which are seen are temporal; but the things which are not seen are eternal.

—*II Corinthians 4:17-18*

THERE is the contentment of a rewarding task in Jacob's toil for Rachel; but in Paul's labor there is ecstasy. Jacob works for Rachel; Paul works for God in Christ. What he calls his "light affliction, which is but for a moment" is in truth a whole life of fierce conflict and crushing adversity. He seems hardly to feel the weight of it, so lost is he in the ocean of God's love at every moment. We used the word "ecstasy." This can mislead us unless it means to us what it should mean. An ecstatic is not really one who goes around in a trance, out of mental touch with the unromantic realities of the world around him; rather he is one who stands outside himself. Paul's ecstasy is such. It gives him a total self-transcendence which delivers him from the pain and weariness of self-concern—the real punishment for sin.

Thus his work is made not only tolerable but joyful. Spinoza well defines joy as the passage from a lesser to a greater perfection. The man who works for something less than God but greater or dearer than self to him—Rachel, or fatherland,

or science, or slum clearance, or any cause outside himself—
enjoys this lesser perfection. It can make his work meaningful,
rewarding, and seemingly easier than it is; it can make the
time fly.

Paul has passed into the greater perfection in which is ful-
ness of joy. Though not a mystic in the later sense of the word,
the Apostle would probably agree with Boehme: "We are all
strings in the concert of God's joy; the spirit from His mouth
strikes the note and tune of our strings." God's joy is in His
unremitting toil for the redemption of the world which He
has "loved and lost a while," and as a partner in the divine
labor Paul enters into God's joy. This "greater perfection" is
open to all men, but only as they give themselves wholly to the
service of God in Christ.

Caught up into this creative joy, Paul sees all the earthly circumstances, which might have made his life a life sentence at
hard labor, as "temporal"—transient, passing, incidental.
What he really lives with are those things unseen which are
eternal—the loving purposes of God, His eternal counsels, and
the everlasting love which Paul knows that he shall live with
through all eternity.

25

Twenty Pieces of Silver

Then there passed by Midianites merchantmen; and they drew and lifted up Joseph out of the pit, and sold Joseph to the Ishmeelites for twenty pieces of silver: and they brought Joseph into Egypt.
—*Genesis 37:28*

JOSEPH is one of the high heroes of his nation's history: a saviour of God's people at a time when they were threatened by starvation. Having risen to the top of the Egyptian state, second only to the Pharaoh, he was able to bring his people down into that fruitful land and so to preserve them from death.

But here we see him when his life isn't worth much more than a nickel; "twenty pieces of silver" is the price put on him—not very much. His jealous brothers have thrown him into a pit as one disposes of the carcase of a dead dog. Some wandering desert ruffians have come upon him, pulled him out, coolly appraised him, and turned him into cash at the nearest slave market. As a slave he makes his ignominious entry to the land where he is to become a mighty potentate.

His brothers, his captors, and his purchasers put a low price on him. And it would be very easy for Joseph to accept this valuation of himself and to make it his own. We do this naturally. Burns in his familiar line regrets that we do not see ourselves "as others see us," but may it not be that the truly regrettable fact is just the contrary— that we do see ourselves as others see us, and that we agree with them? If others put a high price tag on us, we accept the compliment cheerfully and we heartily approve. If others put us in the cheap bargain-counter class, we sadly concede that they are probably right.

The matter becomes worse when, as so often happens, we conclude that the world's valuation of us is God's. Joseph stands before us as a helpful object lesson. He begins his career in Egypt with this thing clear in his mind: man's contempt for him is not God's. This sharp, clear distinction between what men think of him and what God thinks of him is the beginning, the groundwork, of his greatness. The rest is history. He well knew what the world, represented by his brothers and those who bought and sold him, thought of him. He dared to believe that God's valuation would prove different. "He's worth small coin—twenty pieces of silver," said the world. "He is the man to save My people," said God in the final event.

We never know, and we can never learn, God's rating of us until that final event when we have given God a fair chance to use us in the fulfilment of His hidden purposes.

26

Thirty Pieces of Silver

Then one of the twelve, called Judas Iscariot, went unto the chief priests, and said unto them, What will ye give me, and I will deliver him unto you? And they covenanted with him for thirty pieces of silver.
—*St. Matthew 26:14-15*

JESUS was worth just ten pieces of silver more than Joseph, in the price for which He was sold. They were about equally cheap.

It would be easy to exclaim, "How the world's evaluation of Him has changed!" The Christian Church is the world's largest real estate corporation, and it is all in His Name. We have crowned Him with many crowns of art and architecture and expensive philanthropies. Nothing we can build or buy for His service is really good enough, but we are glad to do our best for Him without stinting.

This is one side of the picture, and because it is true we have every right to note it gratefully and happily. But it is not the whole picture. For one thing, a large majority of people do not share in this tribute, but regard Him with indifference, contempt, or unbelief. And for another thing, the true test of our valuation of Jesus is not the money we spend on Him but the devotion we give to Him. This is what He asks of us: that we believe in Him, love Him, follow Him, and obey Him. On this test, do we come out so well?

We can give a lot of money and work to His cause and at the same time we can put a marked-down price on Him. Our commonest way of doing this is to accept Him and to try to use Him as our helper rather than as our Lord and Master. When we do this we follow some such line of reasoning as the following: Christ's religion, in moderate dosage, is good for us, so we'll take as much of it as we think we need. "It calms our sorrows, heals our wounds, and drives away our fears." He can help us, by His noble example, to be more courageous, more patient, more tolerant, more helpful—and at the same time happier. We can forget, or explain away, His stern demands, His hard words, and His extreme claim to be the absolute Lord of our lives by divine right. Perhaps if He had lived in our more enlightened age He would have spoken more moderately and reasonably about Himself, so we will give Him the benefit of the doubt and generously forgive His ancient Jewishness and His other handicaps.

Thus we can still value Him at about thirty pieces of silver —not very much. We can even bear His Name as we put our bargain price upon Him.

27

"And He Was a Luckie Felowe"

And the Lord was with Joseph, and he was a prosperous man.
—*Genesis 39:2*

WHEN William Tyndale translated this verse in 1530 he chose a less dignified phrase than "a prosperous man" to describe Joseph in Egypt. Because the Lord was with him, says Tyndale, "he was a luckie felowe." Since any man hopes that the Lord will make him "a luckie felowe" in this world we need to sit down now and then with this question of what we may expect of God.

Lord Bacon's famous epigram that prosperity is the blessing of the Old Testament and adversity of the New is not entirely accurate. We can find exceptions in the Old Testament to this rule. Yet it is the rule. And it remains the rule among us: to whatever extent we are *B.C.* in our thinking rather than *A.D.*, we see in our prosperity or luck the sign of God's favor, and we see in its absence from us the sign of God's disfavor.

Ought we to thank God for temporal prosperity or success when it comes to us? Certainly. He is the Giver of all good things; and prosperity is a good thing. It is unrealistic and unnecessary to make any pious pretense to the contrary.

Joseph of Arimathea was able to provide a sepulcher for our crucified Lord because he was rich. There are many things the rich man can do for God, or the influential, or the gifted, which the poor or uninfluential or ungifted person cannot do. Joseph was able to save God's people from starvation only because, in Egypt, "he was a luckie felowe." Assuredly the Lord was with him to prosper him and to make this possible.

The author of the 44th chapter of Ecclesiasticus sees the whole truth of this matter. Of the poor and unknown servants of God "who are perished, as though they had never been" he prophesies that "their glory shall not be blotted out." God will see to that. But he has some good words to speak of those servants of God who were rich and famous: "The Lord hath wrought great glory by them through his great power from the beginning. Such as did bear rule in their kingdoms, men renowned for their power, giving counsel by their understanding . . . Rich men furnished with ability, living peaceably in their habitations. . . ." They also serve. As Marcus Aurelius put it, "Even in a palace men can live well."

This is the neglected side of the truth. It is true; but not the whole truth.

28

Poor But Making Many Rich

And a certain scribe came, and said unto him, Master, I will follow
thee whithersoever thou goest. And Jesus saith unto him, The foxes
have holes, and the birds of the air have nests; but the Son of man hath
not where to lay his head.

—*St. Matthew 8:19-20*

WHY did the Son of God choose to be born and to live a
poor man? Part of the answer is the fact that He was
not so poor as we tend to think. He was not a pauper. He grew
up in a home which we should call today middle-class. His fos-
ter father was an independent artisan. Jesus left the security of
home and livelihood when He entered upon His public ministry, but He had a security to leave. He could have lived com-
fortably had He chosen.

Nor have we any warrant for saying that His renunciation of
material security for Himself was a condemnation of material
security as such. Jesus loved those good things of life which
money can buy. The wine and food at the wedding feast in
Cana, the precious ointment with which the sinful woman
anointed His feet, the hospitality of Mary and Martha and His
other friends, and other data in the Gospel story make this
clear.

His own special vocation called Him to a homeless and pen-
niless career. He had to proclaim and to inaugurate the
kingdom of God on earth, and the task was great and His

days were few. Earning a living, keeping up a home, take some of a man's time, and He had not the time for it.

He does not call every disciple of His to give up all worldly goods and security to follow Him. But this He makes very clear: it is what we *are,* rather than what we *have,* that must be our richest offering to God. Material possessions can be devoted to God's service to wonderful effect, but only if we use them and they do not use us.

Christ's great Apostle to the world described the lot of his fellow Apostles and himself as "poor, yet making many rich" (*II Corinthians 6:10*). Their poverty was not an essential part of their calling, but simply an accident of circumstance. It made it possible for them, however, to teach the essential Christian truth by their own example: that our God-given business in this world, be we rich or poor, is to make others rich. We are never prevented from enriching others by our own material poverty. We all have something to give, if the mind of Christ is in us.

29

Joseph and His Brethren

And Joseph said unto his brethren, Come near to me, I pray you.
And they came near. And he said, I am Joseph your brother, whom ye
sold into Egypt. Now therefore be not grieved, nor angry with yourselves, that ye sold me hither: for God did send me before you to preserve life.

—Genesis 45:4-5

THE early Christian Fathers were fond of treating Joseph
as a "type" of Christ, regarding his career as a God-given
sign of the career of the Christ to come. This may seem very
far-fetched to the modern mind, but there is true and valuable
insight in it.

Joseph is rejected and cast out to die by his own. Christ
comes to "his own, and his own received him not." (*St. John
1:11*). God uses Joseph in Egypt as the instrument of a great
salvation of His people. God gives eternal salvation to His
people through the Christ whom they despise and reject. (To
push the parallel into details, the selling of Joseph into slavery
corresponds to the selling of Jesus into the hands of His cru-
cifiers; and Joseph's rise to power in Egypt corresponds to
Christ's rising from the grave to power over the whole universe.)

In the great identification scene (*Genesis 45*) Joseph tells his
repentant brethren that it was not they who sent him into
Egypt but God. That this is the Lord's doing is made plain by

the fact that he is able, as ruler in Egypt, to save his brethren from starvation. Thus God has visited and redeemed His people through Joseph.

But the human fact remains that Joseph came to Egypt because his brothers had cast him out and he had been sold as a slave. The supreme marvel of God's providence is that He is willing and able to save His people through their vile sin of blood betrayal and spiteful cruelty against the innocent.

It is not otherwise in the case of Jesus. God redeems the world by the blood which the world sheds. The mystery of redeeming grace works through the mystery of man's iniquity. Why is it so? Why must a Joseph be sold before a people can be saved? Why must a Christ be murdered by a world before He can redeem that world? It can be only because man's enmity to God makes it necessary for God to work His saving wonders in such ingenious ways—making our evil and sin the instrument of His goodness and love.

But Joseph can save his people only from one evil, and that only for the time being. Another Pharaoh shall arise, who knew not Joseph, and God's people shall become slaves. What the best of men can do for his brethren is only for a moment. Man needs a mightier salvation, which will last forever.

30

Christ and His Brethren

A little while, and ye shall not see me: and again, a little while, and
ye shall see me, because I go to the Father.

—*St. John 16:16*

THE Christ of St. John's Gospel speaks freely and fully of
the consequences of His death before He suffers it. One
of His promises to His brethren is that two times await them:
a time when they shall not see Him, and a time when they
shall see Him "because I go to the Father."

There was a time when Joseph's brethren did not see him,
thinking that they had made a good riddance of him. Then
came a time when they saw him again, in his glory and power;
and this vision of them was their salvation from hunger.

So it is with Christ, however different the circumstances, the
dramatis personae, and the nature of the resulting salvation.

Christ goes to death and the grave, and they see Him not
while He lies in death. Then comes the Gospel's glorious identification scene in the Easter garden. Now they see Him again
and their hearts rejoice. Now they know that He is their Life
forevermore. But even this vision of Him in His Resurrection
is not the final vision. To Mary, in her rapture at beholding
Him again, He speaks those bewildering yet assuring words,
"Touch me not; for I am not yet ascended to my Father: but
go to my brethren, and say unto them, I ascend unto my
Father, and your Father; and to my God, and your God" (*St.*

John 20:17). It is not a threat to remove Himself forever from our sight. It is a promise that His ascension to the Father will raise us to an even higher, clearer, closer, and imperishable vision of Him.

Joseph provides bread for the bodies of his brethren in Egypt —until an unsympathetic Pharaoh turns the refugees into slaves. Joseph is now dead, and powerless to prevent this sad ending of the salvation he had wrought.

Christ can say, "I am the living bread which came down from heaven: if any man eat of this bread, he shall live for ever: and the bread that I will give is my flesh, which I will give for the life of the world!" (*St. John 6:51*). He can say this and He can make good His words. Because He has ascended to the Father and is now on the throne of the universe, we can see Him by faith in this life and by direct vision in the life to come; and He can be the living Bread on which we feed now and forever, giving us a salvation which neither man nor Devil can ever destroy.

31

Jacob's "Nunc Dimittis"

And Joseph made ready his chariot, and went up to meet Israel
[Jacob] his father, to Goshen, and presented himself unto him; and he
fell on his neck, and wept on his neck a good while. And Israel said
unto Joseph, Now let me die, since I have seen thy face, because thou
art yet alive.

—*Genesis 46:29-30*

WE MAY define a *nunc dimittis* as a grateful prayer for
God's permission to die, now that one has seen God's
salvation with one's own eyes. The great *nunc dimittis* is that
of Simeon, which we shall think about in our next medita-
tation. Now we consider an earlier one, that spoken by the
aged Jacob when he sees his son Joseph alive in Egypt.

Ever since Joseph had been taken from him many years before, he had lived by a hopeless hope. He was sure that Joseph
was dead. And yet . . . the body had never been found. It was
impossible that he should be alive; but with God all things are
possible, as Jacob knew so well. This hope sustained him in his
hopelessness.

The universal point of this is that no man is content to die,
entirely content, until he sees his deepest hope for somebody or
something on earth fulfilled. When he has seen this he can depart in peace—not before.

Jacob's was his hope of seeing his favorite son alive. It was
a selfish hope, in the sense that all parental love is selfish. The

loving parent cannot say his *nunc dimittis* until he is assured by his own eyes that all is well with the child whom he leaves on earth.

It is not unfair to Jacob to note that all through the story he manifests more concern for his child Joseph, and for his youngest child Benjamin, than he does for his starving clan as a whole. To the end of his days Jacob remains a man peculiarly wrapped up in "his own." He is narrowly and selfishly possessive. He believes intensely in God, but it cannot be said that his love for all men or even for his clansmen reaches out very widely. Yet the old man's *nunc dimittis* moves our hearts and we rejoice with him as he embraces his beloved son and declares to God that he asks no more of life.

Perhaps the wisest Christian reading of this story is as a reminder that love for those who are peculiarly our own is not enough, all by itself. God knows that we love our own children with a very special love which we cannot give to any others, and He wills it to be so. But our love for one another within the family is meant to be an education in a wider and more embracing love. To love one's own child child rightly is to learn to love every child of God. Our home, as God would have it, is the kindergarten of heaven.

32

Simeon's "Nunc Dimittis"

And, behold, there was a man in Jerusalem, whose name was Simeon; and the same man was just and devout, waiting for the consolation of Israel: and the Holy Ghost was upon him.

And it was revealed unto him by the Holy Ghost, that he should not see death, before he had seen the Lord's Christ.

And he came by the Spirit into the temple: and when the parents brought in the child Jesus, to do for him after the custom of the law,

Then took he him up in his arms, and blessed God, and said,

Lord, now lettest thou thy servant depart in peace, according to thy word:

For mine eyes have seen thy salvation,

Which thou hast prepared before the face of all people;

A light to lighten the Gentiles, and the glory of thy people Israel.

—St. Luke 2:25-32

SIMEON, we assume, had no children of his own and no kindred. His family was God's people Israel, for whose Saviour he looked as his one and only hope. Let him see this hope come in the flesh and he is ready. But will he not want to remain on earth to see the New Age of God, when Messiah is come? Evidently not. Only to see with his own eyes the Saviour actually here is all he asks. Then he can lay down the burden of his long watching and hoping and praying.

There is an unearthly selflessness in old Simeon's hope, as contrasted with the fierce parental exclusiveness of Jacob's hope to see Joseph again. And St. Luke rightly emphasizes the fact that Simeon is not an ordinary man, because "the Holy Ghost was upon him." Jacob, the natural man, and Simeon, the Spirit-filled man, both live for a hope which they cherish in love. But Jacob lives for his precious boy and for nobody else; and do not even the heathen the same? There is no great merit in such parental devotion. The savage has it, and even the tiger.

Simeon's willingness to die from a world in which his people are about to be saved, once he knows that the Saviour has come, is the telltale mark of the Holy Spirit's work in him. The work of the Holy Ghost, as the Prayer Book teaches us, is to sanctify us and all the people of God; and we are sanctified as we are made capable of this pure, selfless devotion to God and His people, to the complete forgetting of self. Simeon ought to be more prominent than he is in the Christian gallery of pre-eminent saints. He has lived, and now he is ready to die, for the salvation of Israel. And his heart's hope runs out beyond the borders of Israel as he sees the Christ who is "a light to lighten the Gentiles" to the saving knowledge of the one true God.

Whenever we want to know precisely what difference the Holy Spirit can make in a human life, we may recall Jacob's *nunc dimittis* and then Simeon's. Here we see the difference.

33

The Gatherer of the People. I.

The sceptre shall not depart from Judah, nor a lawgiver from between his feet, until Shiloh come; and unto him shall the gathering of the people be.

—*Genesis 49:10*

THIS prophecy is part of the great song known as the Blessing of Jacob. The song as a whole is a mosaic of separate tribal oracles which an editor has brought together and has put on the lips of the dying Jacob as his last will and testament to his twelve sons, the progenitors of the twelve tribes of Israel. Judah has a specially high destiny. Not only is he (collectively speaking) to occupy that part of the land which bears his name, the heartland of Israel whose capital is Jerusalem; Judah is to produce the nation's great leaders "until Shiloh come"—the greatest of them all, unto whom "shall the gathering of the people be."

But who, or what, is Shiloh? This is one of the most difficult textual problems in the Bible, and there is no sure solution. Shiloh may be the name of a city. If so, the whole verse should be re-translated. Or it may mean "rest." It can mean "peaceable" or "pacific," and in this case it may refer to Solomon, whose name has the same root.

Whatever the original writer had in mind, however, the significance of the verse for us lies in the fact that it came to be regarded as a prophecy of the Messiah. Both later Jews and early Christians took it as such, and it corroborated their belief that the Messiah of God is (a) of the tribe of Judah, (b) a King of Peace, and (c) a gatherer of the people to himself. To the Christian, Jesus appears as the fulfilment of the prophecy.

We may be quite sure that the original writer of the prophecy had something or somebody else in mind, but this need not trouble us. The author of an inspired prophecy need not have full knowledge of how his prophecy is going to be fulfilled; indeed, he cannot. The meaning of a prophecy is to be seen in its actual fulfilment once that has been given. As for our Christian reading of this ancient tribal oracle, we know that Jesus is of the tribe of Judah, that He is our King of Peace, and that He gathers His people to Himself.

God spoke to Israel through this cryptic word, to put into the hearts and minds of His people the image of a Judean King who would bring peace and unity. Thus God always speaks through His prophets, to plant holy dreams which one day He shall bring to pass.

34

The Gatherer of the People. II.

And one of them, named Caiaphas, being the high priest that same year, said unto them, Ye know nothing at all, nor consider that it is expedient for us, that one man should die for the people, and that the whole nation perish not. And this spake he not of himself: but being high priest that year, he prophesied that Jesus should die for that nation; and not for that nation only, but that also he should gather together in one the children of God that were scattered abroad.

—*St. John 11:49-52*

CAIAPHAS had in mind only one thing: to toss Jesus to His enemies as one might toss a lamb to the wolves to keep them from destroying the whole flock. He "prophesied" quite accidentally and unwittingly; but prophesy he did, as St. John reminds us in his comment. Jesus was to die not only for His nation but for all "the children of God that were scattered abroad" whom He would "gather together in one" by His conquest from the Cross.

Thus in Him the ancient prophecy of *Genesis 49:10* is wonderfully fulfilled, far beyond the wildest dreams of the prophets of old. The prophecy is still in process of fulfilment. Our "Shiloh" has come, and through His Church He is gathering together in one the children of God who are scattered abroad in the wilderness of sin and unbelief and ignorance of God.

Christ's gathering together in one the children of God who are scattered abroad is the only answer to the world's disunity and the only hope for an ultimate unity. Yet this must seem an arrogant claim to the non-Christian, and one which Christian history quite scandalously contradicts. Are Christians themselves "gathered together in one" among themselves? What of all the jangling and jarring sects of Christendom? Are we truly a gathered people? The world has every right to wonder. But our dividedness is not the work of Christ. It is the work of the Devil within the Christian fold. St. Paul says of Christ that "he must reign, till he hath put all enemies under his feet" (*I Corinthians 15:25*); which rightly expresses the truth that although Christ reigns He does not yet entirely rule, even within His own household. This is no weakness on His part. It is inherent in Christ's way of ruling—by the full consent, with the full co-operation, of the ruled. Until we let ourselves be wholly ruled by Him, He cannot finish His work of gathering us and making us all one in Him.

Even so, the divine Gatherer of the people is come; He reigns, and He increasingly rules; and where His rule is complete, His people are one.

35

Man's Eloquence

Naphtali is a hind let loose: he giveth goodly words.

—Genesis 49:21

THE destiny of the tribe of Naphtali is the unusual and most admirable one of being a clan of men who combine beautiful speech with splendid action. "They must have been a very gallant, high spirited people, these members of an ancient clan," Dr. Lynn Harold Hough remarks. "They must have been characterized by a kind of swinging movement and dashing energy. . . . Do you have a vision of a highland country, and moving in the mountains, leaping from crag to crag, a hind which has been in captivity but is finding its way now once more to its native haunts? There is something in the lightness of its limbs, the grace of its movements, the subtle combination of fleetness with sureness and firmness, which fills you with amazed happiness as you watch it moving on the heights. Well, Naphtali is like this, says the poet, 'like a hind let loose.' "[1]

But these men of Naphtali are not only great men of action. They are men of eloquent speech. "He giveth goodly words." And this is indeed a combination rich and rare. Too seldom do we find the man who both speaks well and acts well.

[1] Lynn Harold Hough, *The Church and Civilization.* Used by permission of Round Table Press, Inc., New York.

We have come to be very suspicious of goodly words, and well we may in our fallen world. Goodly words can be spoken by a dunce, as Chaucer reminds us: "A fool can noght be stille." Goodly words can be spoken by a knave. And if they are not used to conceal folly or knavery they may be used as a substitute for deeds. Even that lover of words, Dr. Johnson, must note in the Preface to his Dictionary: "I am not so lost in lexicography as to forget that *words are the daughters of earth, and that things are the sons of heaven.*"

The truth seems to be that we cannot trust our tongues to do their work wisely and well unless we put them under a strict Master. Our own minds and hearts are not sufficient for this. The only adequate master of our words and our works is God. The men of Naphtali, whose words were goodly and whose actions were those of the hind let loose, were men of God. This alone can explain them.

Natural eloquence is a precious gift, but a dangerous one. It needs to be supernaturalized by that communion with God which enhances every natural gift and makes it a blessing and not a curse.

36

God's Eloquence

But when they shall lead you, and deliver you up, take no thought beforehand what ye shall speak, neither do ye premeditate: but whatsoever shall be given you in that hour, that speak ye: for it is not ye that speak, but the Holy Ghost.

—*St. Mark 13:11*

THIS is our Lord's counsel to His earliest disciples as He prepares them for the persecution they will undergo for His sake. It would be easy to misinterpret it, and Christians commonly have done so. The preacher, for example, who enters the pulpit without having given a moment's thought to what he is going to say, trusting in "inspiration," is not obeying Christ's counsel. He is simply coasting on his own laziness.

These men to whom our Lord is speaking are men whom He is calling to a lifelong intimate communion with Him and an absolute self-surrender to Him. If they obey His call they will find that the Holy Ghost, Christ's "Alter Ego," will be with them at all times and in all places to guide them into what they are to say and to do. This is the promise, and it is to us as to them. If we give our lives to this communion with our Lord, His Spirit will act through us and speak through us. Our eloquence will be God's eloquence.

It is the eloquence of the surrendered life whose Ruler and Guide is the Lord. Now, it is abundantly clear from the lives of all the great servants of Christ that the Holy Spirit is the spirit of disciplined intelligence. Consider again the case of the preacher who argues that to prepare a sermon in advance is to betray lack of trust in God's inspiration. He is resisting the truth that when God gives him time and opportunity to prepare what he is to say in God's Name God expects him to use it. He is not in the position of the early Christian who might be dragged out of bed in the dead of night and brought before the magistrate to plead guilty or not guilty to a capital charge.

What is abidingly true is that as we live our lives in unceasing trust in God and reliance upon Him for all that we need, we are given the words He wants us to speak. If He gives us time to premeditate, it is well; then we premeditate under the Spirit's guidance. But even in our untroubled lives there come many moments when we must speak without premeditation. In those moments pre-eminently we show ourselves either under the influence of the Spirit of God or not under it. God's eloquence is given to us only as we give our eloquence, and all that is in us, to God.

37

"I Am." I.

And Moses said unto God, Behold, when I come unto the children of Irsael, and shall say unto them, The God of your fathers hath sent me unto you; and they shall say to me, What is his name? what shall I say unto them? And God said unto Moses, I AM THAT I AM: and he said, Thus shalt thou say unto the children of Israel, I AM hath sent me unto you.

—Exodus 3:13-14

THIS is a mysterious passage, and biblical scholars generally agree that it is comparatively late. The conception of God as the original I AM, as absolute Being, is highly metaphysical and is not likely to have been held by simple nomads of the time of Moses. Certainly it is not primitive theology. To the theologians of later Judaism it probably meant, as Dr. I. G. Matthews suggests, "I am the unquestioned Ruler." But when Dr. Matthews goes on to say that "it is authoritarianism in religion"[1] we get the impression that this good democratic American Christian considers this a fault. "Authoritarianism" is a bad word for a bad thing to most of us. The suggestion that God is "authoritarian" is very distasteful.

In one sense, the God of Moses and of Christ is not authoritarian. The real authoritarian, such as Hitler, will not allow his subject to make any free choice of his own. He will

[1] I. G. Matthews, *The Religious Pilgrimage of Israel*. Used by permission of Harper & Brothers, New York.

coerce not only the bodies of his subjects but their minds and
their wills if he can. Our God does not. We defy or disobey Him
at our peril, but He gives us the power to do so. The most of-
fensive thing about real authoritarianism is that it allows no
such freedom.

If, then, we choose not to think of God as authoritarian we
need not. But he does present Himself to us as "the unquestioned Ruler." He cannot do otherwise and still be God. He
makes us in His own image, but He does not make us little
gods. We have being only because we derive our being from
Him, who is the ultimate Ground of all being. C. S. Lewis
somewhere remarks that God is the only noun and that we are
adjectives. The adjective takes its meaning from the noun. The
word "lovely" says absolutely nothing until it is referred to
some noun, such as "sunset" or "sonata." Our lives say nothing
meaningful and indeed have no meaning until they are referred to God as the Giver of their meaning and the Source
of their being. "John Smith" means nothing. "John Smith,
child and servant of God" is beginning to mean what he is
meant to mean.

God is the only real *I AM*. I am, in a limited and contingent
manner of being, because *He is*.

38

"I Am." II.

Then said the Jews unto him, Thou art not yet fifty years old, and hast thou seen Abraham? Jesus said unto them, Verily, verily, I say unto you, Before Abraham was, I am.

—*St. John 8:57-58*

OUR Lord's Jewish antagonists knew their Scriptures well enough to get the point of His remark. They took up stones to cast at Him for His blasphemy; for His use of the words "I am" links Him in His own being with the divine being of I AM THAT I AM. Some modern theologians make much of the fact that nowhere in the Gospels does Jesus specifically say "I am God." To be sure, His way of affirming His deity is guarded and reserved—for a purpose. He would have us come to know Him as God through our faith in Him and our walk with Him. But in His statement, "Before Abraham was, I am," He makes one clear claim: that He existed "before Abraham was." He claims eternal existence for Himself. If this claim be true, He cannot be less or other than God, for only God has such eternal existence.

The great meaning of this passage for us lies precisely in its assertion that Christ is God, and so we now know in His own Person that God with whom we have to deal. So long as we know God only as the eternal *I AM,* the Ground of all being, the unquestioned Ruler, we know nothing of His purposes for us, His kindness, His love. Now we see Jesus and we hear His *I am;* and we know that the eternal I AM is manifested to us in Him.

Nicolas Berdyaev probably speaks for most of us when he confesses: "The problem of the justification of God in face of the measureless pain in the world has always been a source of infinite torment to me. I cannot admit the conception of an almighty, omniscient, punitive deity beholding this stricken world of ours; I can consent to and understand only the image of a loving, suffering, crucified God; I can, that is to say, only accept God through His Son."[1]

In Christ, I AM becomes human, and shows Himself to us as a God whose final name is not Absolute Being (though He is that) but Love.

[1] Nicolas Berdyaev, *Dream and Reality.* The Macmillan Company, New York, 1951. Used by permission of the publisher.

39

Light from God

And the Lord went before them by day in a pillar of cloud, to lead them the way; and by night in a pillar of fire, to give them light; to go by day and night. He took not away the pillar of the cloud by day, nor the pillar of fire by night, from before the people.

—*Exodus 13:21-22*

THE children of Israel, at the time of their wilderness wan-derings, were a very primitive lot. They were in the nursery stage of their understanding of God and of themselves. Hence they needed guidance—and very obvious guidance. No guid-ance which would require any philosophical acumen or scien-tific skill or spiritual maturity would do for them, for they were not ready for it.

So God guided them by a light they could see: a pillar of cloud by day and a pillar of fire by night. Commentators with a passion for rationalizing such wonders of the Bible suggest that here we have an accurate description of a volcano. It emits a cloud of dust by day and a cloud of fire by night. This may have been Mount Sinai, and the phenomena may well have been those of an active volcano. God could guide them by such a natural sign as well as by a supernatural. It makes no real difference to faith. What matters is that God will give clear guidance to those who trust Him for it; guidance suitable to their capacity to receive and follow it.

One of the tests which must be applied to any religion is this: Does it offer guidance from on high to wayfaring men? It does no good to believe in a God of some kind, or to believe that He has purposes for us, or even to believe that He loves us, if we receive no guidance from Him in the ordering of our way through life. If we feel that we must pick and choose our way for ourselves, in the major crises and the little daily decisions of our lives, without any guiding light from God, we may be sure that our religion is very inadequate.

If we are Christians of the twentieth century *A.D.* we must not expect the kind of "obvious" guidance which God gave to the ancient Israelites, and we should not want it. We should be beyond that kind of thing. Yet one wonders sometimes about some of our Christian contemporaries when they consult horoscopes, or open the Bible at random, or read tea-leaves, in quest of "guidance." All such devices are childish superstitions and a reproach to the God who has given us the very Light of the world to be our pillar of cloud by day and our pillar of fire by night.

40

Light of the World

I am the light of the world: he that followeth me shall not walk in darkness, but shall have the light of life.

—St. John 8:12

JESUS makes this great pronouncement just after healing a woman of moral blindness and just before healing a man of physical blindness. The former malady is much more terrible than the latter. But to all blind souls, whatever their blindness, He offers the Light of God Himself, so that in this Light they may see light, and in His straight path may not stumble.

Apart from Christ, there is no light, no guidance, offered to men by which they can do more than grope their way blindly from one moment to the next. Matthew Arnold's melancholy verdict, expressed in "Dover Beach," is honest realism:

> Ah, love, let us be true
> To one another! for the world, which seems
> To lie before us like a land of dreams,
> So various, so beautiful, so new,
> Hath really neither joy, nor love, nor light,
> Nor certitude, nor peace, nor help for pain;
> And we are here as on a darkling plain
> Swept with confused alarms of struggle and flight,
> Where ignorant armies clash by night.

That closing line is a matchless description of the human swarm in its "natural" state—as it is *B.C.* We are ignorant, for we know not what we do. We are armies clashing, for our fear of the dark makes us fear and hate one another. And we clash by night, in the gross darkness which covers us.

Christ delivers us from that ignorance by showing us that we are sons and daughters of God and that we can fulfil our being by walking in His steps. He cures us of that fear-born hostility to one another by enabling us to love one another—which we cannot do except by His grace. And He rolls back the darkness by being Himself our unclouded Sun.

The follower of Christ makes no pretense that he knows the future any more than does any other man. What gives him confidence and sure-footedness on his way is his awareness that Christ the Light is with him now and will be with him "tomorrow and tomorrow and tomorrow." We do not need to know what is going to happen to us tomorrow, so long as we know that we have as our Guide and Companion One who can deliver us from every evil. No longer do we need a pillar of cloud by day and a pillar of fire by night. Our guide now is not a sign in the skies but a Person, beside us, within us. All that we need to do is to stay with Him.

41

The God Who Hardens Men's Hearts

And I will harden Pharaoh's heart, that he shall follow after them; and I will be honoured upon Pharaoh, and upon all his host; that the Egyptians may know that I am the Lord.

—*Exodus 14:4*

THERE is a fairly common assertion about God in the Old Testament which grates harshly upon Christian ears. It is the suggestion that a wicked man does wickedly because God hardens his heart. In the Exodus story God is constantly hardening the heart of the Pharaoh so that he will afflict the Israelites. This, in turn, gives God an opportunity to save His people from the Pharaoh's clutches. Thus God is "honoured upon Pharaoh, and upon all his host; that the Egyptians may know that I am the Lord."

Does God harden any man's heart to sin, even with this good ultimate purpose of showing forth the divine goodness and power in answer to the sin? We find this very hard to reconcile with what Christ reveals to us of the love of God for all men and His loving desire to save all from sin. God must love the Pharaoh and his host even as He loves Moses and his countrymen.

The people of the Old Testament are ancient Semites, and the strong tendency of all Semitic thinking about God is to attribute *all* things to His direct will and agency. Thus Job,

97

when challenged to curse God because of his afflictions, answers: "What? shall we receive good at the hand of God, and shall we not receive evil?" (*Job 2:10*). Of course the evil comes from Him, because everything does. This is the cardinal assumption in this godly Semite's theology. And on this principle, a man's sin must come from God also. God would not be God if anything happened independently of His sovereign will and decree.

The great Prophets taught Israel to think otherwise, and our Lord completes the instruction which they began. We are sure now that when we sin against God it is not because God has hardened our hearts against Him but because we have hardened our own hearts. At any rate, if we are not sure of this it is because we have resisted the truth that we are responsible for our own sinning and we are trying to blame it on God—or on our bad environment, or our unhappy home life as children, or a vitamin deficiency, or almost anything other than ourselves.

But this much is true in the assertion that God hardens the heart of Pharaoh, or Nero, or Hitler, or any other persecutor of His people: when the evildoer persists in his way, God will have the last word. He did in the case of the Exodus. He always does.

42

The God Who Softens Men's Hearts

I exhort therefore that, first of all, supplications, prayers, intercessions, and giving of thanks, be made for all men; for kings, and for all that are in authority; that we may lead a quiet and peaceable life in all godliness and honesty. For this is good and acceptable in the sight of God our Saviour; who will have all men to be saved, and to come unto the knowledge of the truth.

—1 Timothy 2:1-4

FOR the first three hundred years of their existence in the world, Christians received an almost unrelieved diet of persecution and abuse from "kings, and all that are in authority." It is an impressive fact that the early Church did not appeal to God for revenge upon its persecutors. As Tertullian and others pointed out in their apologies for Christianity, addressed to the civil authorities and the anti-Christian public, the Christians offered constant intercession for God's blessing upon the rulers of the state, even when these were treating Christians as the vilest criminals.

It is clear that Jesus Christ had wrought this profound change, this complete reversal, in the attitude of the godly toward the ungodly. The Old Testament man who believes that God is for him does not hesitate to invoke God's wrath upon the wicked. He comforts himself with the thought of God's vengeance upon his enemy, saying, "I suffer now, but he'll get his comeuppance later."

The new man in Christ does not doubt that God punishes the evildoer, but he has another concern. He yearns and prays for the conversion of the sinner, for in Christ he meets the God "who will have all men to be saved, and to come unto the knowledge of the truth."

As we hear our Lord's injunction to love our enemies and to pray for those who despitefully use us we ought not to take this simply as an exhortation to a noble magnanimity. It is more than that. It is God's asking us for our help in accomplishing His purpose toward these sinners. He wants us to pray for them so that He can use our prayers and our good will as an instrument for the softening of their hearts toward God. How He will do this we do not know. The working of grace in any human life is mysterious. It seems quite clear to us that the sinner's heart cannot be softened toward God unless the sinner himself consents to it. Perhaps God seeks to use our prayers, our patience, and our good will as means of breaking down their resistance.

In any case, Christ reveals to us a God whose concern with the sinner is to convert him; and He calls us to work, will, and pray toward this end and no other.

43

The God Who Fights for Man

And Moses said unto the people, Fear ye not, stand still, and see the salvation of the Lord, which he will shew to you to day: for the Egyptians whom ye have seen to day, ye shall see them again no more for ever. The Lord shall fight for you, and ye shall hold your peace.
—Exodus 14:13-14

NOT many people today believe that God will fight their battles for them without any participation on their part. Our text may seem to suggest that God did this for the Israelites at the Red Sea crossing. We should bear in mind that God had sent them Moses as a leader to call them to a great, dangerous, and costly enterprise. They were not getting this deliverance all for nothing. But this is one crucial moment when it seems that, for this moment, all that they have to do is to "stand still" and to watch their enemies drown.

Thus it is with many a deliverance. God asks us to suffer, to strive, to fight; then comes the crucial moment when the issue is decided for us by some gracious act of God, and all that we need to do is to "stand still, and see the salvation of the Lord."

When Abraham Lincoln was in the White House he received a very pessimistic letter about the woeful state of the Union, from his friend the Governor of Illinois. Lincoln answered with a letter which began: "Dear Dick, Stand still and see the salvation of the Lord." Certainly Lincoln was not sitting back and waiting for God to save the Union, nor was he counseling anybody else to do so. He was simply recognizing that when man is doing his best in God's service he has every right to leave the final issue with God, confidently.

God fights *for* us when we are on His side. Of this we are sure. And He has a wonderful way of giving us the victory when we least expect it and by means which we least expect. But man *B.C.* always hopes that God will do *all* the work. How we should love to do nothing except to sit back, to stand still, to relax, and to see the salvation of the Lord from a box seat! We naturally want Him to do all the thinking, all the work, all the suffering. But He will not have it so.

Our desire for a God who will do all the work for us is one of those childish things which we must put away. God wants us to grow up. And we grow up by sharing with Him the burden of our deliverance from our foes. The highest compliment God can pay us is to ask us to bear a man-size share of that burden.

44

The God Who Fights in Man

I bear in my body the marks of the Lord Jesus.

—Galatians 6:17

THERE is a wonderful buoyancy in all of St. Paul's striving and fighting. Here is a man whose life is eloquent commentary upon the saying of Thomas à Kempis: "They travel lightly whom God's grace carries."

But it would be ludicrous to suppose that Paul simply breezed and coasted to his victories. When he says that he labored "more abundantly than they all," it is no idle boast. When we are tempted to complain of our hard lot we do well to turn to the simple recital of his tribulations in *II Corinthians 11:23-28:* "Are they ministers of Christ? (I speak as a fool) I am more; in labors more abundant, in stripes above measure, in prisons more frequent, in deaths oft. Of the Jews five times received I forty stripes save one. Thrice was I beaten with rods, once was I stoned, thrice I suffered shipwreck, a night and a day I have been in the deep; in journeyings often, in perils of waters, in perils of robbers, in perils of mine own countrymen, in perils by the heathen, in perils in the city, in perils in the wilderness, in perils in the sea, in perils among false brethren; in weariness and painfulness, in watchings often, in hunger and thirst, in fastings often, in cold and nakedness. Beside those things that are without, that which cometh upon me daily, the care of all the churches."

All of these honorable wounds have left their scars upon his body. These he proudly calls "the marks of the Lord Jesus." They show the world that he belongs to Christ. He is a soldier of the Crucified, and the proof of it is visible in his battle wounds. Elsewhere (*Philippians 1:29*) Paul speaks of the *privilege* of not only believing in Christ but of suffering for Him. His reasoning is that if God has high hopes and high regard for us He will give us specially hard and demanding work to do for Him. Hence the very difficulties and distresses which fall upon us in our effort to serve God faithfully are evidence of His loving trust in us.

We are *A.D.*—new creatures in Christ—when we have grown up into this understanding; not before. Our God not only fights for us; He does something more wonderful when we are ready for it: He fights in us, making us not only beneficiaries of Christ's Cross but sharers in it.

45

The God of Limited Jurisdiction

And the Lord was with Judah; and he drave out the inhabitants of
the mountain; but could not drive out the inhabitants of the valley,
because they had chariots of iron.

—Judges 1:19

EVEN the reader with no knowledge of primitive ideas of
God senses that here we have something peculiarly primitive: a belief in a god whose jurisdiction is limited to high
places. So long as his people are fighting against mountaineers
he can help them; but when they come up against the more
civilized folk down in the valley, who have chariots of iron,
he cannot see them through. It may be that this god's territory
is limited to the mountainous district. It may be that he cannot
cope with the technological devices of the people who have iron
chariots. Whatever the difficulty, the god of our text can help
Judah only in one area and against one kind of adversary.

How "primitive" is this conception, actually? In a sense, of
course, it is very primitive. Nobody in Christendom today who
believes in God at all would limit His jurisdiction in quite
this simple manner. But this fear that God's jurisdiction is
severely limited is perennial. It is far from dead.

We meet it in many forms, and perhaps the commonest is
the idea that God has absolute control of the "spiritual" world
but not of the "material" world. Very many people today pray
boldly for spiritual gifts—faith, courage, self-control, charity,

and such, but feel that it is absurd or wrong to ask God for their daily bread or good weather or bodily healing. Clearly they limit God's jurisdiction just as did the author of *Judges 1:19*.

Whether God *can* do a thing is a very different question from whether He *will* do a thing. The fact that God does not give us exactly what we ask for cannot reasonably be taken as evidence that we have asked for something outside His department. Huck Finn tried praying and gave it up as a bad job. "I tried it. Once I got a fishline, and no hooks. I tried for the hooks three or four times, but somehow I couldn't make it work. The line weren't any good to me without hooks. . . . No, says I to myself, there ain't nothing in it." Fishhooks were outside of God's jurisdiction.

We need to understand that *nothing* is outside of God's jurisdiction. Everything is His. He controls everything. It is because He really controls it, and decides what is to be done with it, that it sometimes appears to us that He does not. Our Lord's word concerning this, to which we now turn, should clear up our confusion.

46

The God of the Impossible

With God all things are possible.

—*St. Matthew 19:26*

I T IS well to remember that these familiar words of our Lord are spoken in a definite context and so must be understood in terms of it. He has been talking about the extreme difficulty of a rich man's entering the kingdom of God. He has made it sound virtually impossible; but, He adds, "with God all things are possible"—even the salvation of a rich man. We should not push His "all" too far. There is at least one thing, according to the New Testament, that God cannot do, that is impossible for Him: He cannot deny Himself. He cannot change His own nature. And we are profoundly grateful that it is so. This "impossibility" to God is His unique glory.

Whatever God wills to do He can do. This is the true doctrine of the divine omnipotence, in a nutshell. All things that are desirable to Him are possible to Him. We need never refrain from asking anything of Him on the ground that He is incapable of giving it or doing it.

But as we ask, we need to think; we need to open our minds to the instruction of the Holy Spirit. What if this thing that we are asking of Him could be granted only to the hurt of someone else or to the hindering of God's rule in the world? It is very often so with our desires and petitions. To ask that the law of gravitation be suspended so that I might not break my neck if I fall from a high place is to ask that a law which means life for others be repealed to accommodate me. If God were to do this, it would save my life by destroying other lives. If I am willing to have this done, it is—or should be—quite clear that what I need above all is a new spirit within me; and the God who loves me will be more concerned to give me this than to save my neck.

God is always doing "impossible" things for us. He is always working miracles. But as a rule, if not always, His miracles occur only when somebody acts boldly at God's bidding. An old Jewish legend ingeniously makes this point: "When Moses threw the wand into the Red Sea, the sea, quite contrary to the expected miracle, did not divide itself to leave a dry passage for the Jews. Not until the first man had jumped into the sea did the promised miracle happen and the waters recede."

With God all things are possible indeed; but He gives us the miracles when we give to Him two things: our absolute trust, and our absolute desire that His will, not ours, shall be done.

47

An Unreasonable Sacrifice

And Jephthah vowed a vow unto the Lord, and said, If thou shalt without fail deliver the children of Ammon into mine hands, then it shall be, that whatsoever cometh forth of the doors of my house to meet me, when I return in peace from the children of Ammon, shall surely be the Lord's, and I will offer it up for a burnt offering.
                                                              —*Judges 11:30-31*

JEPHTHAH'S vow ends in tragedy. As he returns from his conquest of the Ammonites, the first living creature to greet him is his only daughter. Because he has made this vow, he must sacrifice his daughter.

The cruel tale is not without its beauty. Jephthah's sense of honor and obligation to God is as great as his heroism in the field. He is filled with the spirit of true godliness and he knows that without God he can do nothing. His daughter's willingness to be sacrificed, so that the vow might not be broken, is beautiful and heroic.

What ails Jephthah is his ignorance of the kind of sacrifice God requires of us; and it is a very common ailment. He is willing to offer to God his most precious possession *outside himself*—his dear daughter. But what God wants is not ours but us: "our selves, our souls and bodies, to be a reasonable, holy, and living sacrifice" unto Him. Jephthah has offered a most unreasonable sacrifice, albeit a most precious one. The true purpose of holy sacrifice is to put ourselves—not our goods as such—at God's disposal. This we shall consider further in the next chapter.

And Jephthah has erred in trying to bribe God. Certainly that is the intent and purpose behind his vow. He says to God, "You do this for me and I'll do that for you." *Do ut des.* He comes to God in a bargain-hunting spirit.

This is always our approach to God until Christ has changed it, and even the Christian must examine himself constantly and relentlessly to see if there be any of this spirit in him as he prays. It can take any one of innumerable forms. "If I go to church and say my prayers, I expect You to give me peace of mind." "If I tithe my income, I expect You to prosper my business." "I will try to love my neighbor as You command if You in turn will make my neighbor my friend and admirer." This kind of bargaining in religion is no different in kind from Jephthah's saying: "I will give You the first living thing that comes out of my door if You will give me victory over the Ammonites."

It is not enough that we make vows and commitments to God, and honor them. They must be good and acceptable in His sight.

48

A Reasonable Sacrifice

For it is not possible that the blood of bulls and of goats should take away sins. Wherefore, when he cometh into the world, he saith, Sacrifice and offering thou wouldest not, but a body hast thou prepared me: in burnt offerings and sacrifices for sin thou hast had no pleasure. Then said I, Lo, I come (in the volume of the book it is written of me) to do thy will, O God.

—Hebrews 10:4-7

THE author of Hebrews sees in this passage from the Psalms (*40:6-8*) the keynote of Christ's life and work. Christ says to the Father: I offer to You, not *things*—however rich and precious—but *Myself.* "Lo, I come to do thy will, O God."

The blood of bulls and of goats is fruitless as a sacrifice to God because it does not involve the offering of our own selves. Even Jephthah's beloved daughter, as an offering, is not Jephthah: and it is Jephthah's life God wants, not his daughter's death.

Christ's whole earthly life is a perfect sacrifice, which is to say that it is a perfect self-offering. He puts Himself, at all times and in all His being, at the Father's disposal. At the age of twelve He declares that He has no business except the Father's business. "My meat is to do the will of him that sent me, and to finish his work" (*St. John 4:34*). This is pure sacrifice, pure offering, the only offering acceptable to God.

And to this self-donation to God are we called in Christ. "I beseech you therefore, brethren, by the mercies of God, that ye present your bodies a living sacrifice, holy, acceptable unto God, which is your reasonable service!" (*Romans 12:1*). So St. Paul exhorts us, and rightly. God invites us to offer to Him all that we are and all that we have. This will not enrich Him, but it will enrich us, and it is out of perfect love for us that He calls us to offer our very being to Him. For He who made us knows that we can never come into our true selves except as we give ourselves to Him; to this end are we born. This is the only reasonable sacrifice, this surrendering of our selves wholly to God's will and service: reasonable because it leads to self-fulfilment.

"I am my own master," said a great Christian, "in the hands of God." He had discovered the truth about his own nature. We are masters of our lives only as our lives are mastered by Him who makes us for Himself. No thing that we possess will do as a substitute offering for our own selves. It is *you* God wants; not *yours*.

49

Our Child

Then Manoah intreated the Lord, and said, O my Lord, let the man of God which thou didst send come again unto us, and teach us what we shall do unto the child that shall be born.

—*Judges 13:8*

MANOAH'S prayer before the birth of his son Samson brings him very close to us. Here is every man's prayer as he faces parenthood: "Teach us what we shall do with the child that shall be born." Only the fool enters into parenthood unadvisedly or lightly. If ever a man prays, it is in this thrilling, yet sobering, crisis.

The prospective parent is gripped by an anxiety which comes from his realization of the paradox that he is responsible for the child's destiny and yet cannot control it. You can bring to bear upon your child's life every good influence, but you cannot make him good. You can have the soundest principles of child-raising and apply them with dedicated constancy from beginning to end, only to have the child turn out to be a total human failure. Is it then your failure? The world says that it is, and your conscience concurs.

Hence our anxiety as we face the coming of our child. Before this crisis is upon us we find it easy to theorize and to dogmatize about how a child should be raised. "If ever I have a child, I'm going to do this and that and thus and so." Very many books on how to raise children, providing "all the answers" for only $2.98, are written by people who have none of their own. The experienced hands at the game of parenthood tend to be more reticent on the subject.

Manoah had never read a book on child psychology. It was just as well; for his child turned out to be a unique child—as every child does. The only authority on how to bring up the unique child is God, and Manoah wisely consulted Him. Florence Nightingale's mother bore a unique child, as all the world knows. The poor woman didn't know what to make of little Florence, and used to complain tearfully to her friends: "We are ducks who have hatched a wild swan." Lytton Strachey lays aside his cynicism for once as he comments: "It was not a swan that they had hatched; it was an eagle."[1]

But whether our duckling is to be a swan, or an eagle, or a dodo, we can do nothing right except as we are taught of God at every step of the way. And the final issue we must leave with Him. We cannot determine it ourselves.

[1] Lytton Strachey, *Eminent Victorians*. Used by permission of Harcourt, Brace and Company, New York.

50

God's Child

And when eight days were accomplished for the circumcising of the child, his name was called JESUS, which was so named of the angel before he was conceived in the womb. And when the days of her purification according to the law of Moses were accomplished, they brought him to Jerusalem, to present him to the Lord.

—St. Luke 2:21-22

JOSEPH and Mary were conforming to the custom of Israel in bringing their Child to the Temple to present Him to the Lord. This custom sacramentally expresses the most fundamental truth of parenthood: that our child is not ultimately ours but God's. In Holy Baptism, Christian parents conform to the same truth. It is regrettable that our baptismal liturgies do not give more obvious and explicit expression to this, but nobody should fail to see that it is there. When the child is made the child of God by God's adoption and grace it is settled that, henceforth and forever, this child belongs not to his parents, but to God.

Probably because we have not sufficiently emphasized this in our teaching, Christian parents generally have gone on treating their children as their own children rather than as God's children. It is right for them to recognize, of course, that God leaves the child in their care for the years of his childhood. But unless they recognize that their task is to raise the child for God, rather than for themselves or for himself, they misuse and pervert the commission God gives them. It is entirely too common a thing to hear a bereaved parent cry, "Why did God take my child from me?" *My* child, *our* child: we take for granted the rightness of such language and such thinking, but we have no right to do so. Once we have presented the child to God in Holy Baptism there should be no further uncertainty as to whose child it really is.

Joseph and Mary themselves may have had trouble keeping constantly and completely in mind the true filial belonging of their Child to God and not to themselves. This seems to come out in the incident of the Child Jesus in the Temple (*St. Luke 2:41-51*). The Child Himself had to teach them. His business was the Father's business. He belonged to God, not to them, even though He was "subject unto them" as He grew up.

Let every Christian parent understand that it is so no less with "his" child. We do not own our children. We simply take care of them and train them for everlasting life in that eternal Family in which we ourselves are children.

51

The Religion of Mere Morality

And Ruth said, Intreat me not to leave thee, or to return from follow-
ing after thee: for whither thou goest, I will go; and where thou lodgest,
I will lodge: thy people shall be my people, and thy God my God.
—*Ruth 1:16*

R UTH is one of the most appealing and lovable people in
the Bible, and to criticize her adversely is to risk making
somebody very indignant. Nothing will be said here to debunk
her reputation for constancy in love, loyalty in friendship,
sweetness in adversity. Let all that stand. But there is something
about her religion that must be cross-examined. When she, a
Moabite girl, says to her Hebrew mother-in-law Naomi, "Thy
God shall be my God," she seems to bracket so momentous a
step as changing gods with such things as changing her address. To be sure, in her world each god had his own territory: Chemosh in Moab, Jehovah in Israel, and so on. But even
in that age there were people who said, "I have only one God,
and I am persuaded that He is the one true God. Wherever I
go, I shall serve Him, and Him only, till my dying breath."
All deep religion says this; and it must be noted that Ruth
does not say it. She loves Naomi; therefore Naomi's home,
Naomi's land, and Naomi's God are all good enough for her.

It can be rightly said, of course, that through her loyalty to
Naomi she was brought to the knowledge of the one true God.
But if Naomi had worshiped the Devil, Ruth would have gone

along with her to her church. Her view is that what matters, in religion and in life, it is to be true to one's friends. What does it matter what we call God—Chemosh, Jehovah, Allah, or the Principle of Cosmic Concretion? What does it matter how we worship Him, what we believe about Him, what is our ritual and our creed, so long as we are good and faithful in our social obligations?

Such seems to be Ruth's philosophy of religion. Be good, sweet maid, and let who will be clever about such matters; or narrow, or orthodox, or fastidious, or deeply concerned about the true Church and the true Faith. And such is the attitude of man *B.C.,* natural man. He is eminently broad-minded, tolerant, and inclusive in his religious outlook. His only dogmatism is his dogmatic intolerance of dogmatism.

Since this philosophy of religion is so respectable today, it is well to remind ourselves that it is strictly *B.C.,* historically and spiritually. Christ does not speak of tolerance. He says, "I am the truth."

52

The Name that Excludes to Include

There is none other name under heaven given among men, whereby we must be saved.

—Acts 4:12

IN ONE of the first Christian sermons ever preached, St. Peter makes it emphatic that the name of Jesus is not the name of just another great seer and prophet sent to us to bring us to God. His is the one necessary name, the only name, by which men *must* be saved. The natural man thinks that this is very narrow bigotry. Certainly it is narrow in the sense that it excludes from our religion anything, everything, that does not conform to Christ. We do not call the mathematician narrow and bigoted when he tells us that the square root of 100 is 10, and that any equation which does not conform to this is false. It is necessarily so with any real truth about anything. If it is true, nothing that contradicts it can be true.

But the significant fact about any truth in its narrow exclusiveness is that by its very excluding it includes. Once we have accepted the mathematician's rigid system in which the square root of 100 must always be 10, and can never be 12 or 3.1416, we are then free to do all sorts of wonderful things with this system which will not permit us to believe whatever we like about numbers.

What is true of mathematical or chemical or biological truth is equally true of religious truth. Once we know that there is no other name under heaven except the name of Jesus Christ whereby we must be saved, we can begin to claim all truth as our own; for whatever is true belongs to Christ. If a truth is spoken by the Buddha, or Plato, or Jeremiah, or Mohammed, or Marx, or Nietzsche, or Darwin, that truth belongs to Christ and is given to us by Him. This is one of the meanings of the New Testament doctrine of Christ as the eternal Word of God: He is the Giver of all truth, in every realm, to man, regardless of who the human middleman may be. No matter that Plato lived before Christ's incarnate life or that Marx was an anti-Christian; if he has been given to see some truth, it is because Christ has shown it to him and wants us to have it.

Whatever truth we know comes from Him. Hence His name includes all truth by excluding all falsehood. This is the narrowness which saves all who will be saved by it.

53

Negative Righteousness

Blessed is the man that walketh not in the counsel of the ungodly,
nor standeth in the way of sinners, nor sitteth in the seat of the scornful.
—Psalm 1:1

THE Hebrew Psalter is traditionally the hymnbook of the
Christian Church, and one can reasonably question the
propriety of this. Some passages in the Psalms are scandalously
sub-Christian. There is here a great deal of self-righteousness
and of trying to curry favor with God. There is almost no trace
of love for one's neighbor, still less of love for one's enemies.

But to raise these objections is to miss the point. The Psalter
expresses, with naked and unblushing honesty, the soul of man
as he honestly feels toward God, his world, and himself. Here
is man *B.C.* pouring out his soul to God; here are we ourselves. And the very inadequacy of what we say to God
through the confessional of the Psalms is a healthy reminder
to ourselves that we need to be redeemed and changed in our
inner being.

We begin with the opening verse of the opening Psalm:
"Blessed is the man that walketh not in the counsel of the ungodly, nor standeth in the way of sinners, nor sitteth in the seat
of the scornful." As a statement of fact, this is unexceptionably
true. If a man is to be a good man, he must begin by ignoring
the advice of the ungodly as to how he should live, by not

letting the sinners all around him carry him along with them, by not taking on himself the role of the moral cynic "in the seat of the scornful."

But is this enough—simply to abstain from evil-doing? The Psalmist evidently thinks that it is. So does the natural man in us. I'll be a good enough man, says he, if I refuse to follow the advice of evil minds, if I refuse to do evil things even though everybody else is doing them, if I refuse to become one of those moral cynics who, as Oscar Wilde puts it, know the price of everything and the value of nothing.

We want to settle, if we can, for such a negative righteousness, a righteousness whose only virtue is that it is not unrighteous. After all, even that is sometimes hard enough, in all conscience. What more can the Lord require of us than to abstain from evil?

The Psalmist thought all this is enough. Naturally we think so too. But so long as we think so we are still *B.C.* Christ comes to tell us that the life most utterly empty of all evil is not enough for God, and must not be enough for us.

54

Positive Righteousness

And he opened his mouth, and taught them, saying, Blessed are the poor in spirit: for theirs is the kingdom of heaven.

—St. Matthew 5:2-3

THUS opens our Lord's great Mountain Manifesto, in which is described the righteousness of those who belong to His kingdom. All Christians who have truly read the Sermon on the Mount find it terrifying. It has been well described as a dress rehearsal for the judgment day. If all this is what the Lord requires of us, how shall any one of us stand before Him? Who is sufficient for these things?

The impossibility of Christ's righteousness as a humanly workable ethic is not our primary concern here, but we should note this essential fact about it: that living up to it can never be a human achievement. It can only be a divine gift. The moment I realize that I cannot make myself heroically humble, compassionate, pure in heart, and all the rest of it, I have taken the first great stride toward the promised blessedness. For knowing that I cannot do this with myself I am in a position to give myself over to God, so that He can do it with me. I cannot make myself humble; I cannot make myself capable of loving my enemies. But the Lord Jesus can.

I am capable, as a natural man with good intentions, of achieving a respectable degree of that negative righteousness we were thinking about in the last chapter, and it is well and necessary that I should. I can keep myself clear of bad principles, bad habits, and moral cynicism, though even for this I need the grace of God. But the only good reason for keeping bad things out of our lives is to create room for the good things which God can give. The positive righteousness of Christ is the full reception of the spiritual gifts of God. The Beatitudes are saying: Blessed is the man who has let God pour into his life the gifts of humility, compassion, meekness, hunger and thirst for righteousness, mercifulness, purity of heart, and the peacemaking spirit.

The first Beatitude is very properly first. "Blessed are the poor in spirit." This means: Blessed is he who knows that he is not wise and good and strong enough to make himself good, and who therefore relies wholly upon God to give him that positive righteousness which alone is sufficient. The man in Christ is not distinguished by the absence of evil in him, but by the dominant and overmastering presence in him of the good which comes from God.

55

Why Are Human Beings Important? I.

When I consider thy heavens, the work of thy fingers, the moon and the stars, which thou hast ordained;

What is man, that thou art mindful of him? and the son of man, that thou visitest him?

For thou hast made him a little lower than the angels, and hast crowned him with glory and honour.

Thou madest him to have dominion over the works of thy hands; thou hast put all things under his feet.

—Psalm 8:3-6

SINCE Copernicus, remarks Bertrand Russell, "it has been evident that Man has not the cosmic importance which he formerly arrogated to himself. No man who has failed to assimilate this fact has a right to call his philosophy scientific."[1] This is substantially true, but we need to remember that long before Copernicus our Psalmist brooded in awe upon the physical vastness of the universe and then asked himself how so little a creature as man can have any importance in the cosmic drama. No thoughtful mind of any age can look at his physical world, whatever his world-picture may be, and fail to be puzzled and troubled by this mystery.

One of the Italian sages expresses one important truth of the matter in the apothegm: "Astronomically speaking, what is

[1] Bertrand Russell, *A History of Western Philosophy.* Used by permission of Simon and Schuster, Inc., New York.

man? Astronomically speaking, man is the astronomer." God has given to man a unique importance in the world by giving him mind. This gift makes him master over other living creatures and even over the interstellar spaces.

This much the Psalmist sees. This much the natural man sees. And it is true and important. But great as this gift of mastery-through-knowledge is, it is not man's greatest gift nor the basis of his claim to supreme importance. Pascal brings us closer to the most essential basis of man's importance and dignity by reminding us of this paradox: "The greatness of man is in that he knows himself to be miserable. A tree does not know itself to be miserable. It is then being miserable to know oneself to be miserable, but it is also being great to know that one is miserable."[2] Walt Whitman had a more cheerful view. He envied the animals of the barnyard and wished that he might turn and live with them, because they do not sweat and whine about their condition and they do not lie awake at night weeping about their sins. What Whitman failed to see is that although the pig is happily incapable of being sad at the thought of his alienation from God, he is unhappily incapable of hoping for reconciliation to God and eternal union with Him.

It is not what man has, but what man hungers and thirsts for, which proclaims his unique importance.

[2] Pascal, *Thoughts*.

56

Why Are Human Beings Important? II.

And he spake this parable unto them, saying, What man of you, having an hundred sheep, if he lose one of them, doth not leave the ninety and nine in the wilderness, and go after that which is lost, until he find it? And when he hath found it, he layeth it on his shoulders, rejoicing. And when he cometh home, he calleth together his friends and neighbours, saying unto them, Rejoice with me; for I have found my sheep which was lost. I say unto you, that likewise joy shall be in heaven over one sinner that repenteth, more than over ninety and nine just persons, which need no repentance.

—*St. Luke 15:3-7*

WHAT makes human beings important? As the Psalmist and Bertrand Russell and all of us must agree, it is certainly not man's commanding physical stature in the universe, for he is a submicroscopic midge. Most people would probably seek the answer in man's intellectual capacity to master his physical universe. And with some reason, for man's intellectual dominion is an ever increasing marvel. But, as Pascal notes, man's unique power of reflection and of self-consciousness is the cause of his unique misery. Man can dream of himself as his Creator intends him to be, and can see the sad contrast between the man that ought to be and the man that is.

It is to man in this misery that Christ speaks, and in such a characteristic Gospel parable as the one we have just read He proclaims the ultimate reason for the importance of human beings. *We are important, not for anything that is in us, but because God loves us.* God does not cherish us because He sees great value in us. Rather, His love for us creates our value to Him. He is not impressed by our wisdom, our cleverness, our beauty, our virtue. A man may love Bach's music because of what he finds in Bach's music. We should not think of God's loving us in any such way.

In other words, He loves us not because we are intrinsically lovable but because He is infinitely loving. This is the Gospel of God as He is in His mind and will toward man. And so, when we have received and assimilated this Gospel, we think of ourselves and our neighbor—even the least of these—as important simply and solely because of our importance to God. God so loves us that He gives His only-begotten Son. We do not make it a "good investment" on His part, by proving ourselves a precious prize to be striven for and won. It is not what is in us; it is what is in Him that makes human beings important.

57

Righteousness on Props

If the foundations be destroyed, what can the righteous do?
—*Psalm 11:3*

THE Psalmist here poses a serious question. What is a good man to do when all the props on which his goodness rests are knocked out from under him? It is possible to be righteous when circumstances favor it. A man can abstain from stealing bread when he has plenty to eat. He can be generous when he has money to spare. He can be law-abiding when his society has good laws and his neighbors are all keeping the laws. He can serve the Lord vigorously when he has good health. But what becomes of his righteousness when its necessary foundations are destroyed?

This is every natural man's question. We naturally take for granted that the good life requires a favorable situation and good means for the living of it. And there is a large element of truth in this—especially if we are thinking of righteousness in terms of what a good man can do with his life by his own will and performance.

Our modern sociology rests upon this assumption. What is the sense, we say, in expecting a child to grow up to be a good citizen in an evil environment? The first thing we have to do is to provide for him the necessary props: a good environment, a good education, exposure to all those influences which can make him good.

As a principle of social planning this is the only one with any health in it. Insofar as we are able to provide the props for righteousness in other people's lives it is our first obligation to do so.

But all the while we need to remember this: that the first, and final, test of our own righteousness is what happens to it when the props are knocked from under it. If we are soundly good people so long as circumstances are on our side, what happens to our goodness if the circumstances change?

This points up one of the flaws in all human goodness which is strictly humanly achieved. A man can be acceptably good, all on his own, if everything and everybody around him make it as easy and as rewarding as possible. But it is a righteousness rooted in sand, and the sand can shift. What then? That is the question; and the natural man with his natural morality has no answer to it.

58

When the Props Are Down

And there shall be signs in the sun, and in the moon, and in the stars; and upon the earth distress of nations, with perplexity; the sea and the waves roaring; men's hearts failing them for fear, and for looking after those things which are coming on the earth: for the powers of heaven shall be shaken. And then shall they see the Son of man coming in a cloud with power and great glory. And when these things begin to come to pass, then look up, and lift up your heads; for your redemption draweth night.

—St. Luke 21:25-28

OUR Lord's language here is apocalyptic, hence alien and baffling to the modern mind. What we need to understand about the situation He describes is that, in one form or another, it is always coming upon us. It is the situation when all the props of righteousness, and ordered living, and peace and security, are down, leaving us in crisis and chaos. The world of nations is just getting into a comfortable groove of international commerce and prosperous peace when an international gangster appears—and all is shot. In personal life, one is just getting himself squared for a long career of happy and fruitful living when sickness or bereavement shatters it all. Then we are left, as Jesus says, with perplexity and fear, and the very powers of heaven seem to be shaken.

It is precisely then, says He, that we are to look up, and lift up our heads, for our redemption draweth nigh. The Son of man appears to us.

There comes a midnight hour, as Kierkegaard puts it, when all men must unmask. We have supposed that we were getting along very nicely with our good living. Everything favored it. All that we had to do was to keep step with our manifest destiny. The powers of heaven helped, by making our circumstances right. But now the props are down.

Christ can come to us with redemptive power and saving effect only when our self-wrought righteousness has been shattered. Until those props have been knocked out from under us, we have inevitably supposed, as human beings, that we were making our own goodness from moment to moment. And it was widening the chasm between God and ourselves. We do not know our need for God so long as we imagine that we are getting along very well without His help. "I need thy presence every passing hour." Who can say that with any meaning when he has no sense of his own impotence and helplessness? If only disaster can bring us to the knowledge of our true condition, it is a blessing indeed, for it makes us ready to be redeemed by Him who cometh when all else goes.

59

When the Godly Are Down to One

Help, Lord; for the godly man ceaseth; for the faithful fail from
among the children of men.

—Psalm 12:1

ALMOST every Christian writer who quotes a famous
dictum of Professor A. N. Whitehead does so with dis-
approval. It is his saying that a man's religion is what he does
with his solitariness. The usual objection to this runs that the
Christian religion, at any rate, is not a solitary religion; it isn't
the flight of the alone to the Alone; it is life in the family of
God with the other children in the family, hence it is by its
very nature corporate and social—always a family affair—
rather than private and individualistic.

The objectors are right about the Christian religion but
wrong, it seems to me, in the construction they put upon
Whitehead's saying. Perhaps he should have said that the *test*
of a man's religion is what he does with his solitariness, for
this, surely, is what he meant; and he was right.

We all find it fairly easy to be Christian in some degree
when we are surrounded by good, faithful, praying, and prac-
tising Christians. But how is it with us when "the faithful fail
from among the children of men"? What becomes of your
Christianity when the godly are down to one—yourself?

This crisis is bound to come upon any fully functioning

Christian now and then, in some form. You find yourself at a party where all the others are clever people who think that the Christian religion is ridiculous: that the Church is full of hypocrites, the clergy are fools, or knaves preying upon the simple-minded, the Commandments of God are primitive tribal morality, we need to be emancipated from the outmoded Christian superstitions and taboos, and so on. The godly are down to one. And you find yourself deeply troubled by the thought that these people are very intelligent and morally very good. May they not be right? Who are you to stack your poor wisdom against theirs?

The natural man depends very largely upon his friends and neighbors for his own religious faith and practice. Left by himself to hold the line he feels not only man-forsaken but God-forsaken. We need something that only Jesus Christ can give us when the burden of our solitariness is upon us and the faithful are far away.

60

The Godly Are Never Down to One

Seeing we also are compassed about with so great a cloud of witnesses, let us lay aside every weight, and the sin which doth so easily beset us, and let us run with patience the race that is set before us, looking unto Jesus the author and finisher of our faith.

—Hebrews 12:1-2

PROBABLY most Christians who know this rousing Scripture think of the "witnesses" as triumphant souls in heaven who watch us from the heavenly stadium as we fight our good fight. On this view, they are witnesses because they witness us, in the sense of watching us. This is part of the meaning, but not all of it. A witness, in New Testament language, is not so much a watcher of the faithful as a professor of the Faith. The primary point of this passage is that we are surrounded at all times by a mighty army of souls, in heaven and on earth, who are "looking unto Jesus the author and finisher of our faith" even as we are looking unto Him, and they are bearing witness to His redemptive power in their lives. There is really very much more of comfort and encouragement in this understanding of the passage, for it meets our need for assurance that the godly are never down to one. Whether they are physically present with us at the moment or not, the witnesses of Jesus Christ are always with us and we with them so long as we, with them, are looking unto Him who is the "author and finisher of our faith."

This is what we mean by the Communion of Saints, and it is one of the most invigorating realities of the Christian life. It means that we are never alone in our good fight and our faithful witness. The whole invincible army is with us.

The solitariness and forsakenness we feel at some moments is an illusion, but one which can be paralyzing unless we know how to meet it. The writer of Hebrews rightly suggests that we are to keep our eyes fixed upon Jesus Himself, with whom our faith begins and in whom it ends. It turns out to be true that as we keep our attention fixed on Him we are given to realize the presence with us of all others, of past ages and the present, whose gaze is likewise fixed on Him. Here is where the devout study of Christian biography can help us. It enables us to see the saints and heroes of Christ, not as pale, wraith-like creatures of pious fancy, but as living companions and fellow witnesses with us in our struggle. Even though we feebly struggle and they in glory shine, the truth is that they had their solitary moments too; but they kept their eyes fixed upon the great Author and Finisher, and what was enough for them is enough for us.

61

Atheism. I.

NOWADAYS we associate atheism with the head. Rightly or wrongly, we say, the atheist thinks his way through to his atheism, he arrives at it by an intellectual process. The biblical assumption about atheism is that the atheist is a knave, who foolishly persuades himself that the God who punishes the wrongdoer does not exist— or, perhaps, is so far away from man's world that one need not worry about His seeing and punishing one's misdeeds.

Both the biblical and modern views are right, and both are needed. There is an atheism of the head, and it must be justly acknowledged that some people of noble moral character profess it. Such a one was the French humanist Littré, aptly known as "the saint who did not believe in God." He may well have been saintly, even Christlike. Still, intellectually he was an atheist. Quite often we hear people say, "There's no such thing as a real atheist. Everybody believes in Somebody, or Something, up there!" There is no foundation at all for this sentimental dogma, and there emphatically are people who do not believe in Somebody or Something up there. This is intellectual atheism, and one must believe that there is much more of it today than in any earlier age.

Then there is the moral atheism of which the Psalmist speaks. We may recall one of the things which Gulliver in his travels noted among the Lilliputians: "The disbelief of a Divine Providence renders a man uncapable of holding any public station: for, since kings avow themselves to be the deputies of Providence, the Lilliputians think nothing can be more absurd than for a prince to employ such men as disown the authority under which he acts." It was excellent logic. If the welfare of the state depends upon the God-fearing righteousness of its rulers, it would be dangerous policy to let atheists hold public office. But men are capable of a happy inconsistency, and that is why there are honorable and even saintly atheists. A man can disavow God with his mind and yet cling to the law and will of God with his heart. A man can live "as ever in the great Taskmaster's eye" without believing in the Taskmaster. Somebody once defined the atheist as "a person with no *visible* means of support." So long as he receives the support from the Source in whom he disbelieves he may be inconsistent; but, thank God, he is supported.

62

Atheism. II.

Then Paul stood in the midst of Mars' hill, and said, Ye men of Athens, I perceive that in all things ye are too superstitious. For as I passed by, and beheld your devotions, I found an altar with this inscription, TO THE UNKNOWN GOD. Whom therefore ye ignorantly worship, him declare I unto you.

—*Acts 17:22-23*

NOT all the people in Athens were "too superstitious" in this obvious sense of having too many gods and altars. There were atheists there too: intellectual and moral atheists. Whether any of these heard Paul on Mars' Hill we cannot know, though it seems a safe bet that some did.

The Apostle noted that men generally "ignorantly worship" the one true God. This can be said of the atheist, whether his atheism be of the head or of the heart. When an atheist wants to do a good deed, he is worshiping God who is the Author of all goodness by acknowledging that goodness has a claim upon him which he ought to obey. His ignorance is of the Source of the goodness. Even the wicked man who says in his heart that there is no God, trying to convince himself that he can sin safely, wants something that only God can give: power, or pleasure, or whatever his desire may be. His ignorance is of the fact that if he tries to seize, by force or fraud, the gifts of God, he can never enjoy them as they are meant to be enjoyed.

God is the unknown God until He is declared to us by

somebody who knows Him, and that was what Paul was in Athens to do. He had come to tell men that there is no need for them to grope around in the dark, "feeling after God," as he puts it later in his sermon. God has come right down to where we are in the person of Jesus Christ. We need not feel after Him, look for Him, guess about Him, try to climb to heaven to reach Him. He comes to us in our own flesh and blood. Here He is, in the Christ who abides with us. "He that hath seen Me hath seen the Father" (*St. John 14:9*). So the coming of Christ puts an end to all need for ignorant worshiping of the unknown God, either as theists or as atheists. Now we can know Him as He is—if we want to know Him.

If we want to know Him: that must remain as the one condition. The knowledge of God in Christ can be very inconvenient and very costly. Once we have it, we can no longer claim ignorance or "honest intellectual doubts" as to the will of God for us. It puts us "on the spot," as we say today. In Unamuno's words, the God who comes to us in Christ denies us peace and gives us glory.

63

Life Measured by Length

He asked life of thee, and thou gavest it him, even length of days for
ever and ever.

—Psalm 21:4

THIS Psalm extols the king whom God has richly blessed.
God has given him "the blessings of goodness," "a crown
of pure gold on his head," victory over his enemies, and all
such good things as a man naturally wants. Above all, God has
given him "life . . . even length of days for ever and ever." Apparently it is assumed that his Majesty is going to live for a
very long time on earth, even if not literally forever. Certainly
the reference is to length of days on earth. This is what "life"
means to this Psalmist: long life, measured by length.

On this principle, it seems that the most blessed man in the
Bible is old Methuselah. He lived to the exceedingly ripe age
of 969. Nobody has ever come close to tying his record. But it
is the only thing we remember about Methuselah. As Mark
Twain remarked: he lived 969 years, but what of that? There
was nothing doing.

If we are honest with ourselves we shall have to confess that
we naturally give more thought to preserving and prolonging
our lives than to enhancing them. We are more troubled by
fear of cancer than by fear of the sin that so easily besets us
and that threatens to mar the quality of our life. We measure

life by length. And from this we sorely need to be redeemed.

It is no answer to our need to say that God has planted in us the desire for self-preservation. Undoubtedly He has; but what can be the purpose of this—to keep us fighting for our lives only so that we can live as long as possible? If this is what God has in mind, He has a much more sensible way of doing it than His present one. He has only to change our bodies in such a way that our natural span will be perhaps three centuries rather than threescore years. Since He does not do this, He must have some purpose other than that of merely prolonging our lives, in giving us this passion for self-preservation.

Christians look for the answer in our Lord's incarnate life. At the earlier stages of His ministry He preserved His own life by refusing to walk into the traps of His enemies. And we have no doubt of the reason: it was not so that He could prolong His days, but so that He could finish His work on earth. If His mind is in us, His purpose is in us as our only purpose in asking God for more time on earth.

64

Life Measured by Finish

When Jesus therefore had received the vinegar, he said, It is finished: and he bowed his head, and gave up the ghost.

—St. John 19:30

WHEN a music critic writes of the concert artist that "somehow his performance lacked finish" we know what he means. The performer had all the possibilities: the talent, the instrument, the right music. But his performance was incomplete; it wasn't finished; he left undone some things that he ought to have done.

It is in this sense of the word "finish" that we are to understand our Lord's dying cry. It was a shout of triumph, not an exhausted sob of relief at the end of an ordeal; for the only completely finished life that has ever been lived on earth was now being offered up in its majestic wholeness to the Father.

There wasn't much length of days in that life. Possibly thirty-three years, little more. But the life had been finished in the all-important sense of having been brought to full completion.

To be in Christ is to measure life by this standard of completeness, not by length of days.

But what makes a life complete?

We have a bad habit which can be cured only by the grace of God: the habit of judging our lives by others, "desiring this man's art and that man's scope." This gives us a false picture of our possibilities from the start. God makes you *you,* not somebody else. If you are a writer, He does not ask you to do what Shakespeare did, or Shaw, or Dickens; He asks you to do what you can do. What you have to do is to offer your talent to God, your time, your energies, and to devote it all to the work He gives you to do—in the time and with the capacities He gives you wherewith to do it. Your life and work will be a finished performance, completed, rounded out, fulfilled, if it is done as an offering of love to Him.

Our Lord's human life was perfectly finished because it was perfectly offered to the Father. He left it to God to set the time limit on it. He left it to God to determine the results. That is what we have to do. This self-offering to God is what makes for "finish" in a life, and it is the only thing that can provide that quality. It is open to anybody. The only test and measure of a life is its finish. Neither the length of our days nor the accolade of our contemporaries is, in the last, divine analysis, of any weight whatever.

65

Archaism

Our fathers trusted in thee: they trusted, and thou didst deliver them.
They cried unto thee, and were delivered: they trusted in thee, and were not confounded.
But I am a worm, and no man; a reproach of men, and despised of the people.

—Psalm 22:4-6

ARNOLD TOYNBEE uses the terms "archaism" and "futurism" to describe two quite unrealistic states of mind. The archaist looks to the past and is hypnotized by what he fondly imagines was the golden age. The futurist dreams of a golden age to come, and dreams of it so fondly and so fatuously that he neglects the tasks and ignores the possibilities of the present. We must agree with Toynbee that both attitudes are bad. There is no health in them. But he would agree with us that there can be such things as a healthy archaism and a healthy futurism.

Most men seem to be archaists by nature, and in the unhealthy sense. In Chapter 11 of this book we gave some thought to this, under the heading of "giants in the earth." Listen to most people talk about the good old days, when they are oppressed by the things they don't like in the bad present days, and you must realize that this is an almost universal nostalgia.

In the verses now before us, the Psalmist is expressing this mood. The first two verses are harmless enough, and could be healthy. He recalls what wonderful things God did for his ancestors in their days. He could take this as a cue to what to expect of God in his own days. The God who preserved our fathers through their tribulations is still in charge of affairs. But this is not the conclusion he draws. "But I am a worm, and no man; a reproach of men, and despised of the people." Is he forgetting that his fathers went through the same experience in the brave days of old? Apparently so. In his backward looking, he has not looked at everything that was back there. So he draws the wrong conclusion. He is complaining that God does not manage things as well as He did in former days. And so, instead of plunging into the battle made bold by the recollection of God's mighty works in times past, he sits down and mopes.

There is nothing better than a sound reading of the past as preparation for the work and the wounds of the present, if it is a sound reading. But a sound reading of the past makes one thing very clear to us: although God gave His victory to our fathers who trusted in Him, they had their moments in which they were "worms," and no men; "a reproach of men, and despised of the people." Unless we see this in history, it is better not to read history at all.

66

Futurism

Verily, verily, I say unto you, He that believeth on me, the works that I do shall he do also; and greater works than these shall he do: because I go unto my Father.

—*St. John 14:12*

AN UNHEALTHY futurism, as we remarked in the last chapter, would be one in which we became so enamored of the "great day coming" that we sat down and waited for it, using today as only a waiting period between yesterday and tomorrow. Our Lord says nothing to give support to any such attitude.

But we cannot be His disciples and have any feeling that our future is all behind us. The best is yet to be, if we are in Him; and a Christian can say that if he is ninety-nine years old and on his deathbed.

Here is His astounding promise, which we can never read without feeling thunderstruck by it: that if anybody believes in Him, "the works that I do shall he do also; and greater works than these shall he do. . . ." Greater works than the raising of Lazarus from the dead? Yes, says Jesus deliberately; greater even than that. To say the least, anybody who believes this believes that he has some kind of future!

All this shall be, says our Lord, "because I go to the Father." Here is the clue to the meaning. Our Lord's ascension to the throne of dominion over the whole universe makes it possible for Him to be with us and in us at all times, in all places, and to work through us greater miracles than He wrought in His incarnate life.

We should know, by this time, that it has been, and is being, fulfilled in Christian history. While Christ was incarnate, it was not possible for His saving mission to extend beyond His tiny nation. Now that He has gone to the Father His voice has gone unto the ends of the world. And another thing: so long as He was with us in the flesh, all His mighty works had to be done directly by Him. Now He does them through us, so we are in it as His instruments, His hands and feet. This is greater than it was before. His missionaries and ministers, His teachers and healers, His preachers and prophets, His sages and saints have done "greater works" than these Gospel miracles because He has gone to the Father and is now able to work through them.

So long as there remains one work to be done for Him, we have a future if we are at His disposal. But that wonderful to-morrow should be beginning today. We have all eternity in which to serve Him; but there isn't a moment to lose.

67

The God Who Gives Peace

The Lord is my shepherd; I shall not want. He maketh me to lie down in green pastures: he leadeth me beside the still waters.

—Psalm 23:1-2

WISELY and rightly does the Psalmist praise his Shepherd-God for those episodes in his life which are green pastures and quiet walks beside still waters. There is nothing in the Gospel of Christ which repeals or supersedes this wisdom. But the Psalmist should be heard all the way through his piece. He anticipates situations in which he will be surrounded by enemies and in which he will walk through the valley of the shadow of death. Unlike many other Old Testament seers, he will not regard the times of trouble as times when God has manifestly abandoned him—the trouble being the proof.

In other words, this Psalmist is in this respect a Christian before Christ, and his understanding of God's goodness and God's obligations to man is beyond that of the ordinary natural man. The natural man would take part of his testimony and leave the rest. He would say that the Lord shows His goodness—and lives up to His obligations as our Good Shepherd—when He gives us the green pastures and the still waters. If the host of enemies or the shadow of death comes upon us, God has failed. His duty as God is to give us happiness and peace. Isn't this what His goodness means? What kind of goodness could do anything else for us?

The mere fact that we live in the Christian era and are professing Christians is no guarantee that we have outgrown this child's view of the divine goodness and what it must do for us if it is indeed good. Any preacher of Christianity knows what will make his preaching popular and generally regarded as "helpful" and "inspiring." He is required to preach, attractively and persuasively, this gospel: that God is good; that He stands ready at all times to give you what you want; that what you have to do is meet His terms and conditions, which He makes delightfully easy and which are as follows. . . .

Here in America, at least, the green pastures and still waters are commonly thought of in terms of peace of mind, security, a happy adjustment to life, effective salesmanship, and even a trim figure. (We now have a book called *Pray Your Weight Away!*)

It is a universally popular gospel, but totally false, if Christianity is true.

68

The God Who Denies Peace

These things I have spoken unto you, that in me ye might have peace. In the world ye shall have tribulation: but be of good cheer; I have overcome the world.

—*St. John 16:33*

THE great gift of God to us, through Jesus Christ our Lord, is peace. "My peace I give unto you," says Jesus; but "not as the world giveth, give I unto you!" (*St. John 14:27*). Clearly, one of the first things we have to do is to get very clear in our minds the difference between God's peace and the world's peace.

The world's peace is that of the green pastures and the still waters: untroubled existence, contentment, ample well-being of body and spirit. As we noted in the last chapter, this is the gift of God when it comes to us, even though we are calling it the world's peace. What we mean by this is that the world is unanimous in calling this tranquility and prosperity peace—and in saying that it is the only thing that can be called peace.

Christ offers no condemnation or even belittlement of such peace. It is noteworthy that some great moral teachers do. The puritan—and often the prophet—tells us that we ought to be ashamed of enjoying such green pastures when they are our lot. "We are not here to dream, to drift"—or even to have a good time now and then. This harsh, joy-killing word is not of our Lord.

None the less, the peace which He offers to us as His peace is different. It is the peace of being with Him in the midst of His travail and His war. He tells us that as His disciples we are sure to have tribulation in this world—not because this is a good thing but because it is inevitable. The world which resists Him resists us if we are with Him. And if peace is a harmonious adjustment to the world around us as it is, then it must be said that the God who comes to us in Christ denies us peace. He denies us the world's peace even as He gives us His peace.

The peace of Stephen before the Sanhedrin and under the crushing stones; the peace of Savonarola at the stake; the peace of Francis in his stigmata, of John Woolman agonizing over the slaves, of Livingstone in Africa, of Niemöller before Hitler: this is the peace of God, given to those who are willing to forfeit this world's peace so that they can fight for Christ's cause and kingdom upon earth. This is the one peace which God definitely promises and will always give. And to this peace we are called.

69

The Lord God of Truth

Into thine hand I commit my spirit: thou hast redeemed me, O Lord
God of truth.

—*Psalm 31:5*

WE INSTANTLY recognize this verse as the word with
which, according to St. Luke, our Lord closed His
earthly life: "Father, into thy hands I commend my spirit."
But if we fail to note one verbal change that He makes we miss
a profoundly important fact. Jesus does not address God as
"Lord God of truth," but as "Father"; and in our next meditation we shall think our way into the meaning of the change
He makes.

For the present, let us try to forget Christ's wording of it
and all that it implies by the word "Father." Suppose that we
do not know God as our Father but that we do know Him as
Truth—which He is.

The natural man realizes in his wisest moments that the
truth is always his friend, but only in his wisest moments.
Truth is of God, he grants; or, if he doesn't like theology, he
will say that truth has always a certain absolute value in it
which falsehood lacks. It is well to know the truth and to
order our lives by it.

But there is such a thing as "the brutal truth"—the inconvenient, the painful, the intolerable truth. Our loved one has

cancer; our beloved country has in it some terrible denial of justice and brotherhood; our precious child in school is detestable to his teachers and classmates; there is some ugly flaw in our own moral nature. Any such truth as this hurts. And we will spend a lot of time and effort in denying it or evading it, considering it as our enemy because it hurts us.

In resisting truth we resist God Himself. To know this is the beginning of all sanity. If a thing really is true, it has the omnipotence of God in it, and to resist it is as futile as to spit at the stars. God is more than Truth. He is Love. And ultimately, when we embrace truth, even though the very touch of it sears and brands us, we shall receive the healing of the love of God. But to embrace the truth when it hurts, to reject the powerful temptation to deny it or to evade it, takes a courageous faith of which the natural man is not naturally capable. We must pray for the grace always to love and welcome the truth and never to fear it.

When this grace is given to us, we are ready to commit ourselves, living or dying, to the Lord God of truth, knowing that by the sting of the truth we are healed.

70

Truth Made Flesh

And when Jesus had cried with a loud voice, he said, Father, into thy hands I commend my spirit: and having said thus, he gave up the ghost.

—*St. Luke 22:46*

And they stoned Stephen, calling upon God, and saying, Lord Jesus, receive my spirit.

—*Acts 7:59*

IF WE set in order these two texts and the preceding one, we see an evolution which is indeed a revolution.

First the Psalmist's: "Into thine hand I commit my spirit: thou hast redeemed me, *O Lord God of truth.*"

Next, our Lord's: *"Father,* into thy hands I commend my spirit."

Finally, St. Stephens': *"Lord Jesus,* receive my spirit."

We noted in our last meditation that it is a great step forward when a man comes to see both the divinity and the ultimate friendliness of truth—when he longs to embrace it and surrender to it even when it hurts. God is truth. Whatever is true is of God. To run away from truth or to resist it is to resist God.

Jesus carries us a long way farther. God, to Him, is not simply truth in all its majestic but grim inexorability. He shows us the Lord God of truth, and shows us that He is not only our inescapable Master; He is our Father. And even if

He lets us hang on a cross He is still our Father, and our pain indicates no diminution of His love for us. It is from the Cross that His Son commends His dying life to the Father's keeping.

Then Stephen adds his word and we take the third great step. "Lord Jesus, receive my spirit."

God is Truth. He becomes incarnate in Christ and teaches us the divine fatherhood. Now God has drawn so close to us in our divine Brother in our flesh, Jesus Christ, that when we speak to Him we are speaking to God. Stephen was not confusing the Father with the Son. He was not saying, "Jesus is all of God that I know." He is saying, however, that if Jesus is with him God is with him. Jesus is the Lord God of truth—made flesh, coming all the way to us where we are.

Some Christians express anxiety about how they should address God. To whom should they address their prayers—to Father, or Son, or Holy Ghost? Ultimately it makes no difference. It is a needless anxiety. There is one God, and He is the truth which inexorably rules all, while He is also the love we see and receive through Jesus Christ, true God and true man.

71

God in Church

We have thought of thy loving-kindness, O God, in the midst of thy temple.

—*Psalm 48:9*

THE Temple on Mount Zion, in which the Psalmist wor-shiped, was a very beautiful house of God. Not only was it physically splendid; for the devout Jew it was filled with the beauty of holiness and the numinous sense of God's immediate presence. The Most High God of heaven and earth was *there*.

So, when the worshiper was in the Temple, he had no trouble thinking of God's loving-kindness to His people. He could hardly think of anything else. In that holy place, God's presence overwhelmed the soul.

There is nothing unique about this in Judaism. Every re-ligion—at least, every religion with a history, every religion which has claimed the hearts of multitudes of men—has its holy places, and our own religion is no exception. To be sure, most Christians realize that God dwells not only in temples made with hands; His presence cannot be confined to any one place. He is everywhere. But it seems to be a law of the soul that unless we meet God somewhere we meet Him nowhere.

Clearly it is a psychological necessity for man in his religion to have his particular local places of meeting with God; and since this is true we may reasonably conclude that God has made us so and that it is right. And what is true of holy places is equally true of holy times, holy words, holy rites, and holy postures. Any place, or word, or song, or physical object, which enables us to realize God's presence and to think of His loving-kindness is vitally and indispensably good.

But if we can think of God's loving-kindness *only* in the midst of His temple we are spiritually in deep trouble. It is undoubtedly easier to say our prayers in our church than to say them on a crowded bus; but until our communion with Him in the one place has grown into communion with Him in any and every place it is true religion only in embryo. Unless it is liberated it must die in the womb.

In some parts of Latin America, native Christians must travel long journeys to get to their churches. As they return to their homes, many of them can be heard crying,"Good-bye, Christ!" More sophisticated Christians can do the same thing, only less honestly and openly. We can sink into that, if we let ourselves.

72

God Everywhere

Jesus saith unto her, Woman, believe me, the hour cometh, when ye shall neither in this mountain, nor yet at Jerusalem, worship the Father. Ye worship ye know not what: we know what we worship: for salvation is of the Jews. But the hour cometh, and now is, when the true worshippers shall worship the Father in spirit and in truth: for the Father seeketh such to worship him.

—St. John 4:21-23

WHICH is the *real* Temple of God in earth, where is the *true* Church: in Jerusalem, as the Jews maintained, or on Mount Gerizim, as the Samaritans fiercely protested? The woman of Samaria spoke for the natural man. Certainly there must be some one place which is the right place for worship, the place where one can be sure of finding God—as over against all the wrong places for worship, in which people think they are getting the real thing but are only deceiving themselves.

Our Lord's reply is pro-Jewish to a point. "Salvation is of the Jews" rather than of the Samaritans since to the Jews is given a true knowledge of God's transcendence of all boundaries and limitations which would make Him present in one place but absent from others. He announces, however, that the hour has now come—with Him—in which the "true worshippers" will know that God is with them in all places, at all times. Special places and times there will continue to be. So long as man remains a creature of time and space and so long as his nature remains what it is, he will need such aids to devotion as hallowed spots, holy days, exalting music, solemn ceremonial, and all such devices as help him to be still and know that God is with him.

Jesus revolutionizes worship by making it our whole offering of our whole life to God, in constant communion and loving self-oblation. In his *Devil's Dictionary,* Ambrose Bierce scornfully defines "ritualism" as "a Dutch Garden of God where He may walk in rectilinear freedom, keeping off the grass." This may not be offered as a constructive criticism, but there is health in it. The purpose of what Christ calls true worship is—lest we forget— not to keep God off the grass of our workaday lives, but to deliver us into His hands as our sovereign Lord of all. Until everything we think, say, and do is offered to the Father, through the Son, and in the Holy Spirit, all our so-called worship is a futile and sinful attempt to confine God to our pretty Dutch garden. It is not Christian worship at all, but ruinous self-deception.

73

Reconciling God to Man

O God, thou hast cast us off, thou hast scattered us, thou hast been
displeased; O turn thyself to us again.

—Psalm 60:1

WHAT is more natural for man in his distress than to
cry thus to God? Things have gone terribly wrong; it
must be that we have done something to offend God; now He
is visiting His wrath upon us—hence these tears; and we must
somehow appease Him and persuade Him to change His
mind and temper toward us before we are utterly destroyed.

God must be reconciled to us. This is the natural, indeed the
inevitable, assumption of guilty man in his suffering. Even
Christians have gone on assuming this, despite the vision of
the true position between God and man which Christ gives
them and which we shall consider in the next chapter. Most
of our Christian thinking about the Atonement has taken for
granted that God must somehow be changed toward us rather
than we toward Him. And so we have supposed that what
Christ did by His self-sacrifice was to offer Himself as a sin-
less substitute to accept the punishment justly due to sinful
man. In this way, it is supposed, Christ placates the wrath of
God and makes the Father realize that somebody has suffered
enough and so He need not be angry at us any longer.

No wonder that a small child, hearing it all explained in

this way, burst into tears and cried out, "I love Jesus, but I hate God!" We have done a terrible wrong to God in ever letting ourselves entertain any such notion.

Yet it seems entirely natural and right that we should try somehow to talk God into changing His mind toward us, in those moments when we feel that our suffering is the token of His just anger. The truth which expresses itself in this feeling is that we are guilty, and that we deserve to be punished. The falsehood in it is the idea that God is "taking out His temper on us" or "getting even." We fall into this error so easily because we suppose that God reacts to our sin as a very self-righteous man would react: with a holy fury.

God's love for us does not blow hot one moment and cold the next. He never changes, and there is never any need for a change in Him. This is one of the hardest lessons we have to learn in this kindergarten of our life with God, and it is indispensable. Until we have learned it we are not headed toward the truth.

74

Reconciling Man to God

And all things are of God, who hath reconciled us to himself by Jesus Christ, and hath given to us the ministry of reconciliation; to wit, that God was in Christ, reconciling the world unto himself, not imputing their trespasses unto them; and hath committed unto us the word of reconciliation.

—*II Corinthians 5:18-19*

THE best way to get the full import of this world-shaking declaration is to read it with an eye to everything that is said. First, "all things are of God." St. Paul does not mean, of course, our sin. This is of ourselves; yet God makes us capable of sin by giving us the power to defy Him. But what is positively affirmed is that all things that must be done to restore us to God must be done by God. We cannot save ourselves. We cannot even want to return to God except as He moves us from within ourselves.

Then, God has already done the reconciling work "by Jesus Christ"; He has come to us in our flesh, bringing to us not only the invitation to return to God under full pardon but the means of doing so. Christ not only shows us the Father who wants us to return; He provides the ways and means of effecting our return, through His Body the Church.

He has given to us Christians "the ministry of reconciliation"—the authority, the command, the commission, to go out into the world in Christ's name and to invite men to receive the reconciliation which we have received. To be reconciled is to be ordained as a reconciler.

"God was in Christ, reconciling the world unto himself." Here is not a God who must be appeased, cajoled, bribed, or otherwise talked into dropping His charges against us and cooling off His just anger. Here is the God who says: "They have made war, but I must make peace." So Christ comes into the world on this reconciling mission, and it is God who not only sends Him but comes in Him and does His reconciling work through Him. He does not impute our trespasses unto us: that is, prosecute us and make us pay for our sin. He has every right to do so in strict justice; but His is the higher justice of an infinite love. The death of the sinner in his sin may satisfy the requirements of justice, but it cannot satisfy the heart of God; for what He wants is *us*. We are His children and He wants us back in His household so that He can get on with His eternal purpose for us.

What it calls for, then, is no change in Him, but a change in us which is no less than a rising from death to life, a being born again.

75

Are We as Good as We Think?

O how love I thy law! it is my meditation all the day. . . . Through thy precepts I get understanding: therefore I hate every false way.

—Psalm 119:97-104

HERE speaks a man who is very good, but not as good as he thinks. This "law" of God which he so ardently loves is not, as modern Christians may suppose, a statute-book containing hundreds of minute and petty prescriptions for the governance of his conduct at every turn. It is a whole way of life, in the largest sense; a way of thinking and doing and living which makes real moral demands upon the man. It is no small achievement to be good according to this standard. This man is good in the sense of fulfilling arduous duties toward God and his neighbor. He would be a good man in our day or in any day.

What is further to his credit is that he enjoys being good. He finds deep delight in the law of God and in trying to fulfil it without any compromise.

He is not simply a pre-Christian Jew of exemplary virtue and piety. He is the natural man trying to be good, succeeding very well as compared to the average man—and congratulating himself upon his success.

He is not as good as he thinks. He has deceived himself about this. "I have refrained my feet from every evil way," he boasts. "I hate every false way." "I have not departed from thy judgments." How can a man dare to make such boasts to the Most Holy God from whom no secrets are hid? He can do it only if he has lived well enough to blind himself to his faults.

Warned by his example, we do well to ask ourselves if we are as good as we think we are: especially if we are as good as our best neighbors and better than most. The surest way to self-deception about our own goodness is the way of comparing our lives with those of other people. It is the most natural thing in the world. And it is almost inevitably fatal to true self-knowledge and clear self-judgment. For unconsciously we choose for the comparison people who are our moral inferiors, people who make us shine by contrast. We come away from the comparison knowing that we are good, as human goodness goes, but fondly and falsely imagining that we are better than we are.

Our very pride in our virtue is the fount and origin of sin, and we fail to see it at all. The one thing certain about us good people is that we are not as good as we think.

76

"In Me Dwelleth No Good Thing"

I know that in me (that is, in my flesh,) dwelleth no good thing: for to will is present with me; but how to perform that which is good I find not. . . . O wretched man that I am! who shall deliver me from the body of this death? I thank God through Jesus Christ our Lord.

—*Romans 7:18, 24-25*

PAUL had lived by the law of the good and godly man for a long time. He had become a renowned master of it, such a one as the Psalmist we have just been thinking about would have envied. But there came a day when Paul learned that he was not as good as he thought.

His vision of Christ shattered his self-righteousness. He did not then cease to believe that the Law of Israel was good: far from it. What he came to see is that a man can never become a good man by the keeping of that, or any other, law of virtue. If the moral law by which we live is one that we can fully live up to, then we shall reach a point in our moral development where we say "I have arrived." That is deadly. But if our code is so high and so hard that we cannot fully live up to it, it will simply condemn us as permanently and incurably bad.

After all, as Paul declares in this great open confession (*Romans 7:14-24*), when the Law sets before me what a good man must actually be, it condemns me by making it brutally plain that I do not measure up. "To will" to measure up to

God's requirements "is present with me; but how to perform that which is good I find not" in my own natural self. For in my natural self "dwelleth no good thing." If there is to be any hope for me, God must give me a whole new self.

When he becomes a Christian he experiences a new birth into a new life in which he finds goodness possible, not by his achieving it but by his simply receiving it from the Lord. What he could never do for himself Christ does for him, and this is expressed with violent eloquence in his words: "O wretched man that I am! who shall deliver me from the body of this death? I thank God through Jesus Christ our Lord."

Christianity is not a religion of reformation but of regeneration; or, as Paul would put it, not a religion of law but of grace. If there is any goodness in us, we haven't achieved it; our Lord has given it to us, and we receive it by living in simple dependence upon Him. Hence no Christian can feel any pride in his goodness. It isn't his achievement; it is God's gift.

77

Are We as Peaceable as We Think?

Woe is me, that I sojourn in Mesech, that I dwell in the tents of Kedar! My soul hath long dwelt with him that hateth peace. I am for peace: but when I speak, they are for war.

—*Psalm 120:5-7*

M ESECH" and "Kedar" are, according to our knowledge of ancient geography, places far apart. It is not possible that the Psalmist was living in the two regions simultaneously. He means that the people he lives among are crude, violent barbarians. They hate peace; he loves it. But he cannot have it, because the moment he speaks a peaceable word they howl for war.

In this man's case, it may have been entirely so. But he exemplifies a very common attitude, to be found in many a man—and many a nation: "I am forced to live among barbarians. I am a very peaceable man (or nation) myself. But the moment I speak a word for peace, they begin to rattle their swords."

Are we as peaceable as we think? We seldom are. We may not want war or conflict, and we may interpret our aversion to that as a genuine desire for peace in us, unfortunately frustrated by those wicked people who continue to make trouble. Every nation in our world today proclaims itself a peace-loving nation: Russia and America, the most powerful, making the pious protestation most loudly. There is nothing necessarily hypocritical in this. Of course America wants peace, and so does Russia. But neither is as peaceable as it thinks. The proof of that is the simple fact that both are waging the cold war.

It must be recognized that until both parties to a conflict want peace and are willing to sacrifice self-interest to the cause of peace there can be none. Hence a genuinely peace-loving nation or individual may be forced to fight. But the first step toward peace must always be self-judgment. Each party must ask himself: What am *I* doing to promote the general discord? After he has answered that question most honestly, and has amended his fault most resolutely, he can then look critically at the enemy.

The attitude expressed by the Psalmist, and by every self-righteous party to a conflict, is unconstructive and fruitless even when it is justified by the facts. To go on complaining "I want peace but those wicked people do not!" is simply to evoke the same lament from their side, in an antiphon which leads to nothing but further trouble. We are not as peaceable as we think until we take another step: that from peace-seeking to peacemaking.

78

The Peacemakers

Blessed are the peacemakers: for they shall be called the children of God.

— *St. Matthew 5:9*

HOW many people have ever heard of the Argippaeans? Only the readers of Herodotus, and they are not many. If we lived in a wiser world they would be better remembered. Here is the Greek historian's note on them: "Each of them dwells under a tree, and they cover the tree in winter with a cloth of thick white felt, but take off the covering in the summer-time." (The meaning of this custom is unknown.) "No one harms these people, for they are looked upon as sacred—they do not even possess any warlike weapons. When their neighbors fall out, they make up the quarrel; and when one flies to them for refuge, he is safe from all hurt. They are called the Argippaeans."

A sacred nation, a people of peacemakers. It appears that they were too good to last. But the fact that their contemporaries regarded them as a sacred people is profoundly significant. The neighboring peoples sensed that the Argippaeans were what all men ought to be—peacemakers.

Rare and few are the true peacemakers; but they are blessed, says Jesus, because they are the true children of God. They share their Father's character and they do His work.

What characterizes the peacemaker and distinguishes him from the mere peace-seeker is his different purpose. His aim is not "holding his own" or safety or survival, but reconciliation. He faces the fact of the conflict; he will never say peace where there is no peace. But he faces also the fact that the conflict will not be genuinely resolved if one side—even the right side—conquers the other. The true objective is to reconcile the enemies to each other, and there is no peace until this is done. It is not enough that the Allies conquer the Axis, or that the West conquers the East, or that Mary Smith gets the better of John Smith in the divorce court. The only victory is reconciliation. And if we ourselves are involved in the strife, our peacemaking requires of us full repentance for our share of the guilt—and full forgiveness of the other's share.

We are not as peaceable as we think until we rise to this, and we can rise to it only by the grace of God. This is our heavenly calling in Christ, and we must not flatter ourselves upon our peaceableness if the only thing that can be said for us is that we want peace. Even the heathen do the same.

79

Are We as Humble as We Think?

Lord, my heart is not haughty, nor mine eyes lofty: neither do I exercise myself in great matters, or in things too high for me. Surely I have behaved and quieted myself, as a child that is weaned of his mother: my soul is even as a weaned child.

—Psalm 131:1-2

LITTLE Jack Horner's familiar exclamation of awe and delight at his own goodness, as he pulled out the plum, is about the last word in cozy self-satisfaction. Our Psalmist in this passage joins the happy company of those who are impressed by their own virtues. The virtue of which he is especially proud is his humility. If you wonder how in the world one can be proud of humility you have every right to wonder, since pride and humility are incompatible. But some people seem able to bring if off. Are we as humble as we think?

There is a story of a Carthusian monk who was explaining to somebody the peculiar ethos of his order. He conceded that the Carthusians could not match the Jesuits for learning, or the Franciscans for good works, or the Dominicans for preaching; but, said he, "when it comes to humility—we're tops!"

The self-deception involved in this comes easily to anybody, and that is why we need to examine ourselves thoroughly and constantly for any trace of it. We readily confuse some things with humility. The Psalmist boasted that he did not exercise himself in great matters or in things too high for him. The Christian can easily say: "I don't go in for extremes in my religion: I don't spend a lot of my time fasting and praying, and I don't wrestle with heavy theology. I just take what I can handle." He may think this is humility. It is sloth and indifference, in most cases. He calls his vice by the name of a great virtue and takes pride in his fictitious humility.

We can refuse to think, and call it humility. We can refuse to reach for more than we can presently grasp and call it humility. We can pursue a course of prayer, devotion, and discipleship which would not tax the spiritual resources of a turnip and call it humility. We can thank God that we are not as the real servants of God are, and call it humility. We can call anything humility that enables us to sink and settle into a comfortable rut. But if what we want is the truth, we shall realize that humility is not something we can sink and settle into; it is a high and holy summit to be scaled.

80

The Steep Ascent to Humility

Yea, all of you be subject one to another, and be clothed with humility: for God resisteth the proud, and giveth grace to the humble. Humble yourselves therefore under the mighty hand of God, that he may exalt you in due time: casting all your care upon him; for he careth for you. Be sober, be vigilant; because your adversary the devil, as a roaring lion, walketh about, seeking whom he may devour.

—I Peter 5:5-8

THIS characteristic New Testament passage on humility expresses the true nature of the virtue as Christians understand it. It is a fighting virtue, found only in those who are locked in battle with the Devil and who have found that they cannot fight in their own strength. Their humility is their absolute dependence upon God to supply them with the strength to do things impossible to themselves alone. Hence they do not sink into it; they rise to it, and the ascent is steep and hard.

It is only as we work, struggle, suffer, and fight to serve our Lord to the utmost that we can receive humility. It is only as we discover by bitter experience what St. Peter had discovered when he forsook his Lord—that we do not have it in ourselves to follow Christ on our own resources—that we can grow into humility. For humility, negatively defined, is lack of trust in ourselves. Positively defined, it is absolute trust in the Lord and in the power of His might rather than our own.

There is a story of a young man on his first exploit of mountain climbing. After he had reached the top of a high and dangerous mountain he leaped to his feet with a shout of joy in his achievement. But his guide pulled him down with the warning: "Don't do that! The wind will blow you off. You stand on this peak only on your knees!"

We stand on the peak of the Christian life only on our knees. Until we know this, in theory and in practice, we are strangers to humility.

It takes great courage to be humble in this Christian sense. No sluggard, no coward, is capable of it. When Nietzsche complained that Christian humility is "slave morality" he revealed his blindness to the real thing. Carlyle is right in saying: "Odinism was *Valour;* Christianism (*sic*) was *Humility,* a nobler kind of Valour." If a man does not think that it takes valor to cast all of one's care upon God, in the midst of a terrible struggle, it is because he has never done so, or tried to do it, himself.

We have no power of ourselves to help ourselves, but our sufficiency is of God. To know this, and to live by it, is humility; and it is the victory of the valiant in the Lord.